A Portrait of

BELGIUM

BELGIË
BELGIQUE
BELGIEN

Foto's Photos Photographs Aufnahmen
Vincent Merckx

Teksten Textes Text Texte
Georges-Henri Dumont
de l'Académie royale de Langue et de Littérature françaises

A Portrait of

BELGIUM

BELGIË

BELGIQUE

BELGIEN

VINCENT MERCKX
EDITIONS

NOORDZEE

MER DU NORD

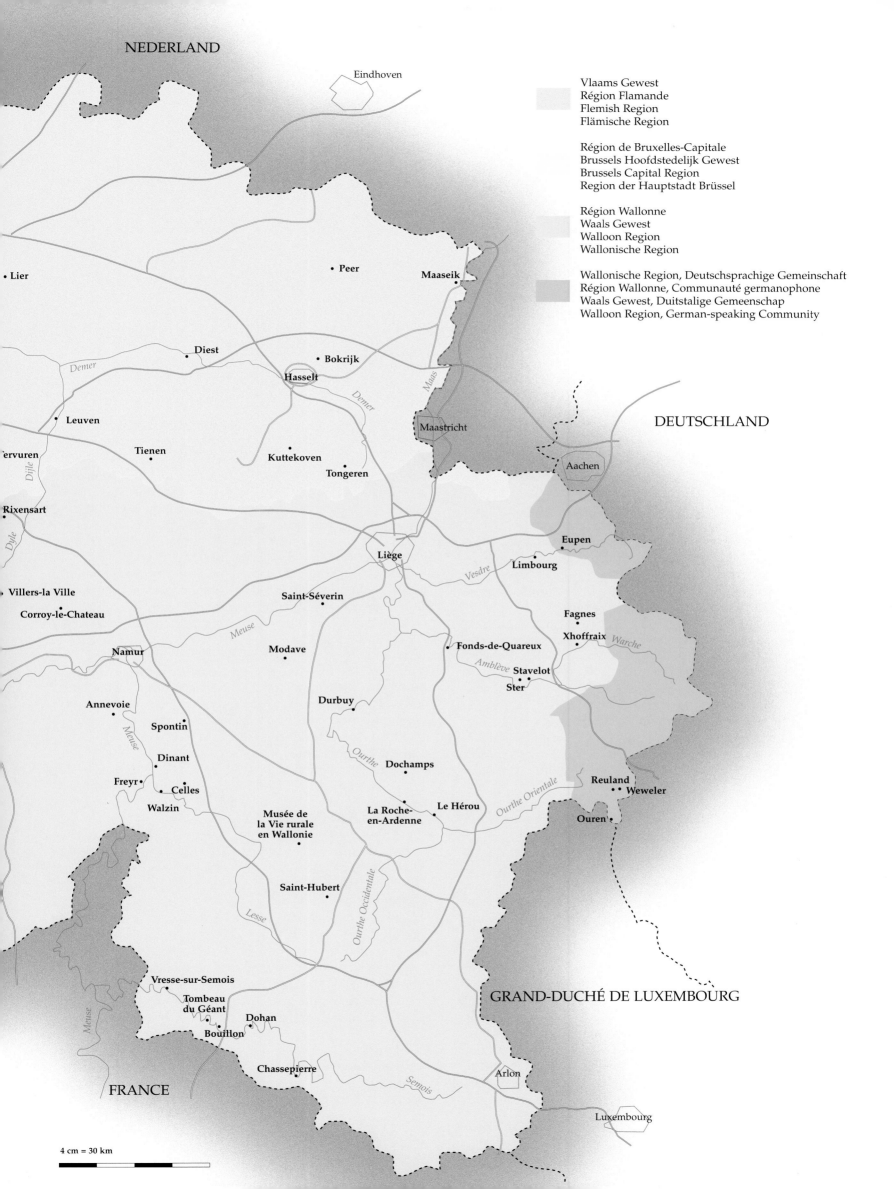

NEDERLAND

Eindhoven

Vlaams Gewest
Région Flamande
Flemish Region
Flämische Region

Région de Bruxelles-Capitale
Brussels Hoofdstedelijk Gewest
Brussels Capital Region
Region der Hauptstadt Brüssel

Région Wallonne
Waals Gewest
Walloon Region
Wallonische Region

Wallonische Region, Deutschsprachige Gemeinschaft
Région Wallonne, Communauté germanophone
Waals Gewest, Duitstalige Gemeenschap
Walloon Region, German-speaking Community

• Lier

• Peer

Maaseik

DEUTSCHLAND

Diest

• Bokrijk

Demer

Hasselt

Demer

Maas

Leuven

Maastricht

Aachen

Tervuren

Tienen

Kuttekoven

Dijle

Tongeren

Rixensart

Liège

Eupen

Vesdre

Limbourg

Villers-la Ville

Saint-Séverin

Dijle

Corroy-le-Chateau

Fagnes

Xhoffraix

Warche

Meuse

Modave

Fonds-de-Quareux

Namur

Amblève

Stavelot

Ster

Annevoie

Durbuy

Spontin

Meuse

Ourthe

Dinant

Dochamps

Freyr

Reuland

Weweler

Celles

Le Hérou

Ourthe Orientale

Walzin

Musée de
la Vie rurale
en Wallonie

La Roche-
en-Ardenne

Ouren

Saint-Hubert

Ourthe Occidentale

GRAND-DUCHÉ DE LUXEMBOURG

Lesse

Vresse-sur-Semois

Tombeau
du Géant

Dohan

Bouillon

Meuse

Chassepierre

Arlon

Semois

FRANCE

Luxembourg

4 cm = 30 km

Wie in België bergop rijdt, komt haast onvermijdelijk in een bos terecht; rijdt hij bergaf, dan staat hij weldra voor de zee. De afstanden zijn maar kort. Nauwelijks heeft de reiziger de kuststreek verlaten, of hij zit al in het Vlaamse binnenland, waar de dorpen samensmelten, zodat er kleine steden ontstaan. Ten zuiden van het bekken van Samber en Maas is het landschap doorsneden met zandsteenhoudende en evenwijdig met elkaar lopende vouwlijnen, die er uitzien als rimpels op een voorhoofd en die de beboste heuvelruggen van de Condroz aankondigen. In de Famenne zijn er rivieren die ineens onder de gespleten rotsblokken verdwijnen en via grotten met echogewelven lager in de valleien weer uit de grond opborrelen. Even verder beginnen de Ardense hoogten, een soort schilddak langs de Duitse grens, dat na een aantal aanlopen op verscheidene plaatsen een hoogte van meer dan 600 m boven de zeespiegel bereikt alvorens het wordt voortgezet door de Eifel. Beken en rivieren worden er meer dan eens door heuvelkammen gedwongen zich in allerlei vreemde bochten te wringen om zich een weg te banen. Het bos van Anlier is de laatste uitloper van de Ardennen. Het steekt boven het land van Gaume uit en weert de noorden- en noordwestenwinden. Wij bevinden ons reeds in de meest zuidelijke uithoek van België, waar de trapsgewijs aangelegde wijngaarden zich in de zon koesteren. En toch liggen Virton en Oostende slechts 300 km van elkaar!

Twee grote waterwegen, de Schelde en de Maas, doorstromen België noordwaarts. Al twee millennia lang hebben ze banden tussen de oeverbewoners gelegd, saamhorigheidsgevoel doen ontstaan en de uitstraling van grote culturele stromingen in de hand gewerkt.

De Schelde is de laaglandrivier bij uitstek. Aan haar oevers ontstond de dynastie van de Merovingers, die haar machtspositie in Doornik verstevigde, alvorens ze naar Parijs trok om daar haar kans te wagen. Ten tijde van de Romaanse kunst verliep de beïnvloeding in tegenovergestelde richting en werden onze streken beïnvloed door Frankrijk. De in Doornik en Soignies (Zinnik) opgerichte religieuze bouwwerken waren toen de opmerkelijkste van het hele Scheldebekken en dragen allebei kentekenen van de toen voor Normandië typische bouwtrant.

De kathedraal van Doornik stond op haar beurt model voor talrijke godsdienstige bouwwerken in de Vlaamse contreien — voornamelijk in Gent en Brugge — en in Brabant. Eeuwen later, ten tijde van de triomftocht van de gotiek, ontstond er eveneens een Scheldegotiek, die haar eigen kenmerken wist te bewaren, terwijl ze zich meer en meer openstelde voor invloeden uit het Maasgebied. Dat de Schelde bovendien aan de wieg van Antwerpen en zijn haven stond, hoeft geen betoog.

De Maas is, in tegenstelling tot de Schelde, een dochter van de bossen. Het Maasbekken werd het machtscentrum van de Pepijnen, die de Merovingers opvolgden en onder Karel de Grote het christendom tot op de oevers van de Elbe deden zegevieren. Dit had een toename van de Germaanse invloeden tot gevolg. Notker, de eigenlijke stichter en prinsbisschop van Luik, was een door keizer Otto I benoemde Zwaab. Het hoeft dan ook niemand te verbazen dat de St.-Janskerk volgens het octogonale grondplan van de paltskapel te Aken werd gebouwd.

Toen nam de eeuwenlange, diepgaande culturele dialoog tussen Rijnland en Maasvallei een aanvang.

De heirbaan van Keulen op Boulogne, later op Brugge, was sedert de oudheid een belangrijke oost-westverbinding, die de contacten tussen Schelde- en Maasvallei in hoge mate bevorderde, vooral toen de handelaars te Brugge de productie van de plaatselijke lakenwevers opkochten en er Engelse evenals Spaanse wol, Oosterse specerijen en andere handelsartikelen invoerden.

In België zijn er verhoudingsgewijs meer steden dan in om het even welk ander land ter wereld. Dit houdt natuurlijk verband met de bevolkingsdichtheid (327 inwoners per vierkante km). Elke stad heeft haar eigen cachet, dat o.a. bepaald wordt door haar oorsprong en rivaliteiten die ooit tussen steden hebben bestaan, maar ze hebben ook een gemeenschappelijk verleden dat gekenmerkt is door een zelfde streven naar vrijheid en zelfbestuur.

De ligging van de Belgische vorstendommen, de bloei van de steden en gelijkgerichte belangen leidden tot de sluiting van vaak onbestendige verbonden. Het waren voorboden van de «federatieve» vereniging onder de hertogen van Bourgondië (van het Huis Valois) en vooral onder Filips de Goede (1419-1467). De door dit vorstenhuis gelegde banden werden als het ware nog meer kracht bijgezet door de schilders, beeldhouwers, bouwmeesters, componisten en schrijvers van deze «Gouden Eeuw», die de groeiende verstandhouding en het eigen karakter van deze beschaving op Europees vlak vertolkten. We vermelden slechts enkele namen: de gebroeders Van Eyck, Rogier van der Weyden, Hans Memling.

Door zijn huwelijk met Maria van Bourgondië, de enige dochter van de in 1477 te Nancy omgekomen Karel de Stoute, kwam Maximiliaan van Oostenrijk en meteen ook het Huis Habsburg in de lage landen aan de macht. Deze europeanisatie ging aanvankelijk gepaard met een haast ongeëvenaarde luister. Ten tijde van Karel V (1500-1555), die de XVII Provinciën aan alle vormen van buitenlandse inmenging onttrok, was het land het rijkste van Europa. Antwerpen, de ontmoetingsplaats van duizenden kooplieden en bankiers, van tientallen kunstenaars en geleerden, verdiende terecht de metropool van West-Europa genoemd te worden.

De diepgewortelde gehechtheid aan de vrijheden — de godsdienstvrijheid en de andere — leidde tot de opstand tegen het eigenmachtig optreden en de onverdraagzaamheid van Filips II met als gevolg het uiteenbarsten van de XVII Provinciën in twee stukken: de calvinistische Verenigde Provinciën in het noorden (nu het Koninkrijk Nederland) en de katholieke Zuidelijke Nederlanden (nu België en Luxemburg). In deze Zuidelijke Nederlanden volgden buitenlandse heersers en bezetters elkaar op, maar de soms door periodes van economisch herstel onderbroken eeuwen van oorlog en vernedering brachten ook een versterking van de wederzijdse banden tussen de verschillende streken met zich mee. Ook op artistiek en literair vlak bleef de vlam branden. De werken van Brueghel en Patinier in de 16de, die van Rubens, Van Dijck, Jordaens in de 17de en die van de prins de Ligne en Grétry in de 18de eeuw bewijzen het ten overvloede.

Alhoewel oorspronkelijk niemand de breuk tussen de XVII Provinciën had gewild, bracht de gescheiden ontwikkeling geleidelijk aan een vervreemdingsproces op gang, dat door godsdienstige verschillen en tegenovergestelde handelsbelangen werd aangewakkerd. De vertegenwoordigers van de mogendheden die Napoleon hadden verslagen, begingen dan ook een flater van formaat, toen ze tijdens het Congres van Wenen (1814-1815) besloten Noord en Zuid samen te voegen en er het Verenigd Koninkrijk der Nederlanden van te maken. Niettegenstaande zijn economische voordelen was dit onvrijwillige huwelijk niet bestand tegen de uiteenlopende karakters van de huwelijkspartners en de onhandigheid van Willem I. Toen de gemeenschap van goederen vijftien jaar had geduurd, brak de Revolutie van 1830 uit en kon het zegevierende Belgische volk eindelijk een streep zetten onder een eeuwenoude strijd. Het vormde een onafhankelijke staat en koos als regeringsstelsel de grondwettelijke en parlementaire monarchie.

De eerste Belgische historici lieten niet na de buitenlanders terecht te wijzen die het nieuwe België als een zuiver formele constructie beschouwden. De meest begaafde onder hen, Jean-Baptiste Nothomb, tevens politicus en diplomaat, schreef in zijn 'Historische en politieke verhandeling over de Belgische Omwenteling' : «De Belgen hebben weliswaar meer dan twee eeuwen lang voortdurend onder de heerschappij van één of andere buitenlandse mogendheid geleefd, maar niet uit eigen wil. Dit blijkt uit het feit dat ze, alle buitenlandse overheersing, ten spijt hun eigen aard hebben bewaard. Spanje is er niet in geslaagd ze te verspaansen, noch Oostenrijk om er Oostenrijkers, noch Holland om er Hollanders van te maken. In de 16de eeuw kwamen de Belgen in opstand tegen Spanje, in de 18de tegen Oostenrijk, in de 19de tegen Holland. Als het waar was, zoals sommigen beweren, dat dit volk geen eigen nationaal bewustzijn heeft, hoe is het dan die vele tegenslagen te boven kunnen komen? Als het geen eigen volkskarakter, geen eigen nationaliteitsgevoel heeft, waarom heeft het zich dan niet door een vreemde natie laten inlijven? Twintig jaar nadat het voor de Franse militaire overmacht was gezwicht, heeft het zelfs Frankrijk een blauwtje laten lopen. Napoleon kwam zoals Lodewijk XIV was gekomen : België ploegde voort. Het kon zich verlustigen in het zien voorbijtrekken van alle vlaggen, hoe roemrijk en met eeuwenoude luister omhangen ze ook mochten wezen, het schiep zijn eigen vlag in plaats van die van een ander land tot de zijne te maken.»

Leopold van Saksen-Coburg-Gotha, de eerste koning der Belgen (1831-1865), beperkte er zich niet toe de jonge Staat op een stevige internationale grondslag te vestigen. Deze «vingervaardige geest», zoals Metternich hem noemde, was één van de scheidsrechters van het Europa van zijn tijd.

Leopold II (1865-1909) maakte van zijn land de vierde belangrijkste economische macht ter wereld. Hij vond het land te klein voor de onstuimige industriële bedrijvigheid van zijn bevolking. Daarom belastte hij ze met de bescherming van het hart van Afrika tegen de slavenhandel en met de ontginning ervan. Belgisch Kongo bleef een kolonie tot in 1960, toen België het gebied spontaan zijn onafhankelijkheid verleende.

«Het meest kwetsbare land ter wereld» werd door twee wereldoorlogen geteisterd. In 1914 deed het Belgisch leger onder de leiding van koning Albert I, in 1940 onder het bevel van Leopold III soms veel meer dan zijn plicht en kwam het alle internationale verplichtingen na.

Na de Tweede Wereldoorlog ging België onder de regering van koning Boudewijn geleidelijk aan en soms met horten en stoten over tot een federaal staatsbestel. De drie Gemeenschappen — de Vlaamse, de Frans- en de Duitstalige — en de drie Gewesten — het Vlaamse, het Waalse en het Brussels hoofdstedelijk Gewest — hebben nu een ruim zelfbeschikkingsrecht wat betreft de materies waarvoor ze volgens de hervormde grondwet bevoegd zijn. De tijdens het Franse bewind ingevoerde, monolithische, sterk gecentraliseerde staatsstructuur heeft het veld geruimd voor een structuur die meer rekening houdt met de eigentijdse werkelijkheid en het pluralisme op cultureel vlak. Zoals koning Boudewijn naar aanleiding van de nationale feestdag op 21 juli 1993 in zijn politiek testament verklaarde, kunnen deze nieuwe, vrij ingewikkelde instellingen slechts goed werken, als de Belgen blijk geven van «federale burgerzin». De nieuwe, zesde koning van het land, Albert II, heeft ter gelegenheid van zijn troonsbestijging op 9 augustus 1993 eveneens daarop gewezen.

Tegelijkertijd heeft België actief deelgenomen aan de internationale ontwikkeling. Het trad toe tot de economische unie van de Benelux, werd medestichter van de Verenigde Naties en de daarvan afhangende gespecialiseerde instellingen en werd bovendien lid van de NAVO, die na de terugtrekking van Frankrijk haar hoofdzetel in België is komen vestigen. België is eveneens één van de zes oprichters van de Europese Gemeenschap voor Kolen en Staal en ondertekende het Verdrag van Rome al in 1957. Dit verklaart waarom Brussel nu nog niet rechtens, maar toch feitelijk de hoofdstad van de Europese Gemeenschap is, die nog steeds, o.a. ook met het Verdrag van Maastricht, op een vollediger eenwording van Europa aanstuurt.

En Belgique, les routes montent vers la forêt et descendent vers la mer. Rapidement, car les distances sont très courtes. À peine a-t-on quitté les plages du littoral que déjà l'on pénètre en Flandre intérieure, où les villages se soudent les uns aux autres pour former de petites villes. Au sud du sillon Sambre-et-Meuse, une série de bandes gréseuses annoncent les crêtes boisées du Condroz. En Famenne, les rivières se perdent, pénètrent dans les roches fissurées, s'engouffrent dans les «chantoirs» pour réapparaître au fond des vallées comme de nouvelles sources. L'Ardenne est proche. Telle un bouclier relevé vers l'Allemagne et s'y prolongeant par l'Eifel, elle se soulève en vagues successives et se maintient par endroits à plus de six cents mètres d'altitude. Les rivières se heurtent à des arêtes rocheuses et se replient en méandres capricieux. La forêt d'Anlier marque la fin de l'Ardenne; elle surplombe la Gaume et lui assure la protection contre les vents du nord et du nord-ouest. Nous sommes à l'autre bout de la Belgique. Il y a même des vignes qui s'étagent au soleil. Mais quelque trois cents kilomètres à peine séparent Ostende de Virton.

Deux grands fleuves navigables — l'Escaut et la Meuse — traversent la Belgique du sud au nord. Au cours de deux millénaires, ils n'ont cessé d'unir leurs riverains, d'engendrer des solidarités et de charrier les grands courants culturels.

L'Escaut est par excellence le fleuve de la mer et c'est sur ses rives, à Tournai, que la dynastie mérovingienne se créa et se renforça avant de s'orienter vers Paris. À l'époque de l'art roman, le mouvement se fit dans l'autre sens : les influences prépondérantes s'exercèrent à partir de la France. À Tournai encore et à Soignies s'élevèrent les monuments religieux les plus significatifs du domaine scaldien, l'un et l'autre apparentés à l'esthétique normande. Très vite la cathédrale de Tournai fit souche et ses rameaux se développèrent dans la plaine flamande et en Brabant, singulièrement à Gand et à Bruges. Le courant scaldien se maintint toujours aussi puissant à l'âge du gothique, mais avec une originalité de plus en plus accusée et une évidente perméabilité au courant mosan.

Faut-il le dire ? C'est à l'Escaut qu'Anvers doit sa vocation portuaire.

La Meuse est, dans sa majeure partie, le fleuve de la forêt. Dans son bassin naquit la dynastie des Pippinides qui prit le relais de celle des Mérovingiens et, sous le règne de Charlemagne, dilata la chrétienté jusqu'à l'Elbe. Il en résulta, par la suite, une large ouverture aux influences germaniques. Le prince-évêque Notger, le véritable fondateur de la grandeur de Liège, était un Souabe nommé par l'empereur Otton Ier, et c'est tout naturellement que l'église Saint-Jean fut édifiée sur le plan octogonal de l'église palatine d'Aix-la-Chapelle.

Pendant des siècles, un intense dialogue culturel se poursuivit entre la région rhénane et la région mosane. Facteur décisif, dès l'Antiquité, de relations continues entre les bassins de la Meuse et de l'Escaut, une route les traversa d'est en ouest. Elle relia Cologne à Boulogne et, plus tard, à Bruges, dont le port fut hanté de marchands qui chargeaient la production locale de draps et déchargeaient les laines d'Angleterre et d'Espagne, les épices et les produits de l'Orient.

Plus que nul autre pays au monde, la Belgique est une terre de villes. Cela s'explique assurément par la densité de la population : 327 habitants par kilomètre carré. Chaque ville a son caractère propre, hérité de ses origines diverses et de ses rivalités anciennes, mais les principales ont en commun un passé marqué par la volonté d'autonomie et la soif de libertés.

La position géographique des principautés belges, le développement économique de leurs villes et la convergence des intérêts rendirent indispensable la conclusion d'alliances successives. Celles-ci constituent la préface au rassemblement «fédéral» entre les mains des ducs de Bourgogne et singulièrement de Philippe le Bon (1419-1467). Et, comme pour renforcer la solidité des liens établis par la dynastie, peintres, sculpteurs, architectes, musiciens et écrivains de ce «Siècle d'Or» donnèrent à l'Europe culturelle le témoignage d'une mentalité commune et d'une civilisation originale. Qu'il nous suffise de citer les peintres van Eyck, Rogier van der Weyden, Hans Memling.

Par le mariage de Marie de Bourgogne, fille unique de Charles le Téméraire, mort à Nancy en 1477, avec Maximilien d'Autriche, les «bas pays au bord de la mer» passèrent à des souverains de la Maison de Habsbourg. Il en résulta une européanisation qui, à ses débuts, fut d'un éclat exceptionnel. Sous le règne de Charles Quint (1500-1555) qui libéra totalement les XVII Provinces de l'emprise étrangère, le pays continua d'être le plus riche d'Occident. Hanté par des milliers de marchands et de banquiers européens, mais aussi des dizaines d'artistes et de savants, Anvers mérita incontestablement le titre de Métropole de l'Occident.

Mais l'attachement viscéral aux libertés — les religieuses et les autres — entraîna la révolte contre l'autoritarisme et l'intolérance de Philippe II. Il en résulta le déchirement des XVII Provinces en deux entités : les Provinces Unies calvinistes du nord (les futurs Pays-Bas) et les Pays-Bas méridionaux catholiques (la future Belgique et le Luxembourg). Se succédèrent alors des souverains étrangers et des occupants. Mais ces siècles de guerres et d'humiliations, jalonnés de périodes de reprise économique, resserrèrent les liens entre les provinces méridionales. Ils ne tarirent pas la source de création artistique et littéraire. Bruegel et Patenier au XVIe siècle, Rubens, van Dyck et Jordaens au XVIIe, le prince de Ligne et Grétry au XVIIIe en témoignent à suffisance.

Bien qu'involontaire en ses origines, la rupture des XVII Provinces provoqua la formation progressive au nord et au sud de mentalités différentes, de divergences religieuses et de rivalités commerciales. Aussi bien, au Congrès de Vienne de 1814-1815, les puissances victorieuses de Napoléon se trompèrent lourdement en décidant que les Belges et les Hollandais formeraient le Royaume-Uni des Pays-Bas. Ce mariage imposé comportait de grands avantages économiques mais il ne résista pas à des incompatibilités d'humeur, jointes aux maladresses du roi Guillaume Ier. Quinze années après sa conclusion, ce fut la révolution victorieuse de 1830. Les Belges touchaient enfin au but de nombreux siècles de lutte. Ils s'organisèrent en un Etat indépendant et choisirent le régime de la monarchie constitutionnelle et parlementaire.

Les premiers historiens belges ne manquèrent pas de réagir contre ceux qui, à l'étranger, présentaient la neuve

Belgique comme un État conventionnel. Jean-Baptiste Nothomb, le plus talentueux d'entre eux — homme politique et diplomate, par ailleurs — écrivit en 1833, dans son Essai historique et politique sur la Révolution belge : « Si, depuis plus de deux siècles, l'histoire nous montre les Belges constamment à la suite d'un autre peuple, cette condition n'a jamais été de leur choix : ce qui le démontre, c'est qu'à travers toutes les dominations étrangères, ils sont restés eux-mêmes. L'Espagne n'a pas réussi à les rendre espagnols, l'Autriche, autrichiens, la Hollande, hollandais. Au XVIe siècle, ils ont fait une révolution contre l'Espagne, au XVIIIe contre l'Autriche, au XIXe contre la Hollande. Si, comme on le prétend, ce peuple ne renferme pas en lui-même aucun principe d'existence, comment se fait-il qu'il ait résisté à tant de catastrophes ? S'il n'a pas de nationalité propre, pourquoi n'a-t-il pas accepté de nationalité étrangère ? Il n'a même pas voulu de la France qui ne l'a possédée vingt ans que par la conquête. Il s'est tu devant Napoléon comme il s'était tu devant Louis XIV; il les a laissés passer. On a déployé sous ses yeux tous les drapeaux; il y en avait de brillants, il y en avait sur lesquels étaient inscrits des siècles de gloire; il n'a adopté aucun des drapeaux. Il s'en est fait un à lui-même. »

Élu premier roi des Belges par le Congrès national, Léopold de Saxe-Cobourg-Gotha (r. 1831-1865) ne se contenta pas d'asseoir solidement la position internationale du jeune État belge; « esprit manipulateur », comme disait Metternich, il fut l'arbitre de l'Europe de son temps.

Sous le règne de Léopold II, de 1865 à 1909, la Belgique se haussa au rang de quatrième puissance commerciale du monde. Estimant son sol trop étroit pour la débordante activité industrielle du pays, Léopold II lui donna le cœur de l'Afrique à défendre contre les marchands d'esclaves et à mettre en valeur. Le Congo fut colonie belge jusqu'en 1960, date à laquelle la Belgique lui donna spontanément l'indépendance.

Les deux guerres mondiales n'épargnèrent pas « le pays le plus exposé de la terre ». En 1914, sous le commandement du roi Albert Ier, et en 1940 sous celui du roi Léopold III, l'armée belge fit son devoir, remplissant intégralement les obligations des traités internationaux.

Au lendemain de la Seconde Guerre mondiale, sous le règne du roi Baudouin, la Belgique s'est engagée — non sans difficultés ni heurts — dans un processus de fédéralisation qui assure désormais aux trois Communautés — flamande, française et germanophone — et aux trois Régions — flamande, wallonne et de Bruxelles-Capitale — une large autonomie de gestion dans les matières que leur ont attribuées les réformes constitutionnelles. Elle a ainsi rompu avec la centralisation d'un État unitaire, héritée de l'occupation française et ne correspondant plus aux réalités d'un État pluriculturel. Selon les mots du roi Baudouin dans son message-testament du 21 juillet 1993, le bon fonctionnement de ces institutions relativement complexes postule un « civisme fédéral ». Le roi Albert II, devenu sixième roi des Belges, en a rappelé la nécessité dans son discours inaugural du 9 août 1993.

En même temps, le pays s'est efforcé de jouer un rôle international actif. Partie prenante de l'union économique Benelux, membre fondateur de l'Organisation des Nations-Unies et des autres institutions spécialisées du système de l'O.N.U., il est intégré dans l'Organisation du Traité de l'Atlantique Nord dont il abrite le siège. De la Communauté européenne du Charbon et de l'Acier, la Belgique fut l'un des six membres fondateurs; elle le fut aussi de la C.E.E. à Rome en 1957. Tout naturellement, Bruxelles réalise sa vocation de capitale de fait, sinon de droit, de l'Europe de l'après-Maastricht.

△
*Het Koninklijk Kasteel van **Laken**.*
*Le château royal de **Laeken**.*
*The Royal Castle of **Laeken**.*
*Das Königsschloss in **Laken**.*

(Double page suivante)
***Weweler**. Son église à haut toit d'ardoise est merveilleusement posée sur la colline. La tour massive date du XIIIe siècle.*

(Volgende dubbele bladzijde)
***Weweler**. De kerk met haar hoge leien dak overkoepelt als het ware de heuvel. De massieve toren dateert uit de 13de eeuw.*

(Next two pages)
***Weweler**. Its church, with its high slate roof, is poised on the hill. Its massive tower dates from the 13th century.*

(Nächste Doppelseite)
***Weweler**. Die Kirche mit ihrem hohen Schieferdach krönt den Hügel auf sehr harmonische Weise. Der wuchtige Turm stammt aus dem 13. Jh.*

In Belgium the roads rise rapidly towards the forest and descend as rapidly towards the sea, for the distances are very short. Hardly has one left the coast than one is in the heart of Flanders where the villages straggle into one another to form little towns. South of the Sambre and Meuse line a series of sandstone ridges, as parallel as a furrowed brow, announce the wooded crests of the Condroz. In Famenne rivers disappear into rocky clefts, plunging into underground watercourses, only to reappear elsewhere as new rivers. The shield of the Ardennes lifts towards Germany where it continues as the Eifel. It rises in successive waves to reach more than 600 meters in some places. The rivers are deflected by these rocky outcrops and meander back and forth in the depths of the forest. The Antier forest marks the end of the Ardennes, protecting the Gaume from the north and north-west winds. We are now on the far side of Belgium where there are even vineyards. And yet, only some 300 kilometers separate Ostend and Virton.

Two great navigable rivers — the Scheldt and the Meuse — cross Belgium from south to north. During two millenia they have served to unite the people dwelling on their banks, to provide a social focus and to disseminate broad cultural currents.

The Scheldt is, above all, the river of the sea and it is on its banks, at Tournai, that the Merovingian dynasty arose and consolidated before turning towards Paris. During the Romanesque period the movement was reversed, the most important artistic influences coming from France. The most imposing religious architecture of the Scaldian region, related to the Norman style, was built at Tournai and Soignies.

The style of Tournai cathedral took root rapidly and branches were developed in the Flemish plain and in Brabant, particularly at Ghent and Bruges. This Scaldian style continued to dominate during the Gothic period, acquiring an even more marked originality due to Mosan influences.

And of course the pre-eminence of Antwerp as a port is due to the Scheldt.

The Meuse is, for the greater part, the river of the forest. In its basin rose the family of the Pepins which later seized power from the Merovingians as the Carolingian dynasty. Christianity spread as far as the Elbe, resulting in Germanic influences. Prince-Bishop Notger, the true architect of the grandeur of Liège, was a Swabian appointed by Emperor Otto I. Thus it is not by chance that the church of Saint John is built on an octagonal plan similar to the Palatine chapel in Aachen. Over the centuries there were intense cultural exchanges between the regions of the Rhine and the Meuse.

A very important factor, dating from antiquity, was the close relationship between the basins of the Meuse and the Scheldt due to the road running from east to west, linking Cologne to Boulogne. It was later extended to Bruges which imported the wool of Spain and England, as well as spices and goods from the Orient, and exported the local cloth.

The population density of Belgium — 327 inhabitants per square kilometer — makes it a highly urbanized country. Each town has its own personality, formed by its local history and traditional rivalries, but the largest ones have in common a past marked by the desire for liberty and independence.

These communal liberties and exemptions were often extended in the provincial charters, notably the one that Duchess Jeanne of Brabant and her husband Wenceslas of Luxemburg were forced to grant at their Joyeuse Entrée of January 3, 1356.

The geographic position of the Belgian principalities, the economic development of their towns and other common interests made successive alliances necessary. These were the prelude to the « federal » system of the Valois Dukes of Burgundy, particularly under Philip the Good (1419-67) the « Founder of Belgium ». As if to emphasize the strength of the union established by the dynasty, a « Golden Age » of painters, sculptors, architects, musicians and writers presented Europe with a distinctive culture demonstrating a common mentality and a unique civilization : the van Eyck brothers, Hans Memling, Roger van der Weyden.

When Mary of Burgundy, the only child of Charles the Rash who died at Nancy in 1477, married Maximilian of Austria, the « low countries on the edge of the sea » passed to the House of Hapsburg. The result was a Europeanization which, at its beginning, was of exceptional brilliance. Under Charles the Fifth (1500-55) who freed the Seventeen Provinces completely from foreign domination, the country was the wealthiest of the Occident. Not only thousands of merchants and European bankers, but dozens of artists, scholars and scientists made Antwerp the acknowledged Metropolis of the West.

However, this deep-seated attachment to liberty, both religious and civil, led to the revolt against the autocratic and intolerant Philip II. As a result the Seventeen Provinces were torn asunder, forming the Calvinist United Provinces in the north — the future Holland, or Netherlands — and the Catholic Low Countries in the south, the future Belgium and Luxembourg. Thence succeeded a series of foreign rulers and occupants. However, these centuries of war and humiliation, mitigated occasionally by periods of economic recovery, strengthened the bonds between the southern provinces. Literary and artistic creativity was never stifled, as is seen by Breughel and Patenier in the 16th century, passing by Rubens, Van Dyck and Jordaens in the 17th, to the Prince de Ligne and Grétry in the 18th.

Although at the beginning the scission of the Seventeen Provinces was felt as a calamity in both the north and south, there gradually arose different mentalities, based on religious differences and commercial rivalries. Thus it was that after the defeat of Napoleon, the victorious powers at the Congress of Vienna (1814-15) were gravely mistaken when they decided that the Belgians and the Dutch would form a United Kingdom of the Low Countries. This forced marriage presented great economic advantages but could not withstand personal animosities as well as the heavy-handedness of King William I. Fifteen years after the union came the successful revolution of 1830. The Belgians finally achieved their goal after centuries of struggle, organizing an independent state under a constitutional monarch and a Parliament.

The first Belgian historians reacted strongly to those

foreign writers who considered the new Belgium as an artificial state. The most talented among these historians was the politician and diplomat Jean-Baptiste Nothomb who wrote in his Historical and Political Essay on the Belgian Revolution of 1883 « Even though more than two centuries of history have shown the Belgians constantly under the tutelage of another people, this has never been by their own choice. What can be demonstrated is that despite all this foreign domination, they have remained themselves. Spain could not make them Spanish, nor Austria Austrian, nor Holland, Dutch. In the 16th century they revolted against Spain, in the 18th against Austria, in the 19th against Holland. If, as is claimed, this people does not have any real claim to exist, why did they withstand so many catastrophes? If the Belgians do not have a true nationhood, why did they not accept a foreign one? They even resisted the French who held them for twenty years by conquest. They endured under Napoleon as they had under Louis XIV. Flags were unfurled before them, many of them brilliant and glorious, but they adopted none of them. They made their own flag. »

Leopold of Saxe-Cobourg-Gotha (reigned 1831-65), elected the first King of the Belgians by the National Congress, was as Metternich said, « a master manipulator ». He not only consolidated the international position of the young Belgian state but established himself as one of the arbiters of Europe at that time.

During the reign of Leopold ll (1865-1909), Belgium rose to become the fourth commercial power in the world. Feeling that Belgium itself did not present enough scope for the abundant industrial energy of his citizens, he gave them the heart of Africa to develop and to defend against slavery. The Congo was Belgian until 1960 when it was granted freely its independence.

The two World Wars did not spare « the most vulnerable country in the world ». In 1914, under the command of King Albert I, and in 1940 under King Leopold III, the Belgian army did its duty, fulfiling international treaty obligations.

After the Second World War, under King Baudouin, Belgium began the difficult process of federalization which will henceforth ensure a greater autonomy to the three linguistic communities — Flemish, French and German — and the three regions — Flanders, Wallonia and Brussels Capital — in the domains specified by the constitutional reforms. The state has thus broken with the centralizing policies of a unitary state, a heritage of the French occupation which no longer corresponded to the realities of a multicultural state. The late King Baudouin, in his valediction on the occasion of the Festival of the Dynasty, July 21, 1993 said that to function properly these complex institutions postulated « federal public-spiritedness ». King Albert II, the sixth King of the Belgians, also stated this necessity in his inaugural address of August 9, 1993.

At the same time the state has continued to play an active international role. Member of the Benelux economic union, founding member of the United Nations and other specialized bodies of the U.N., it is also part of the North Atlantic Treaty Organization and hosts its headquarters. Belgium was one of the founding members of the European Coal and Steel Community and also of the E.E.C. in Rome in 1957. Brussels continues its vocation as the de facto, if not titular, capital of post-Maastricht Europe.

△
*La salle des séances du **Sénat** date de 1849. Le peintre tournaisien Louis Gallait décora les murs de l'hémicycle d'une galerie de portraits de ceux qui ont contribué à la formation de la Belgique, depuis Pépin de Herstal et Charlemagne jusqu'à l'impératrice Marie-Thérèse.*

*De vergaderzaal van de **Senaat** werd in 1849 ingericht. L. Gallait uit Doornik beschilderde de muren van de halfronde zaal met een reeks portretten van de stichters van België vanaf Pepijn van Herstal en Karel de Grote tot en met keizerin Maria-Theresia.*

*The **Senate** chamber dates from 1849. Louis Gallait, an artist from Tournai, decorated the walls of the hemicycle with a portrait gallery of those who contributed to the formation of Belgium, from Pepin of Herstal and Charlemagne to Empress Maria Theresa.*

*Der Plenarsaal des **Senats** wurde 1849 gestaltet. L. Gallait schmückte die Wände des halbrunden Saals mit Porträts der Gründer Belgiens von Pippin von Herstal und Karl dem Großen bis zur Kaiserin Maria-Theresia.*

Wer in Belgien bergauf fährt, befindet sich nach kurzer Zeit in einem Wald; fährt er talwärts, dann steht er auf einmal vor der Nordsee. Die Entfernungen sind kurz. Kaum hat man das Küstengebiet verlassen, ist man schon mitten in Flandern, wo die nahe beieinander liegenden Dörfer kleine Städte bilden. Südlich des Beckens von Samber und Maas kündigt eine Reihe parallel verlaufender, runzelartiger Sandsteinschichten in der Landschaft die bewaldeten Höhen des Condroz an. In der Gegend der Famenne verschwinden die Bäche im gespaltenen Felsgestein, tosen in «Schalltrichtern» und quellen in anderen Talschluchten wieder hervor. Schon sind wir in der Nähe der Ardennen. Wie ein nach Deutschland hin gewölbter Schild gehen sie allmählich in die Eifel über und erreichen in ihrem stufenmäßigen Aufstieg stellenweise eine Höhe von mehr als 600 m über dem Meeresspiegel. Die durch Gebirgsrücken aufgehaltenen Bäche schlängeln sich in bizarren Windungen durch das alles beherrschende Gebüsch. Der Wald von Anlier ist der letzte Ausläufer der Ardennen. Er überragt die Gaumer Gegend und schirmt sie gegen Nord- und Nordwestwind ab. Wieder sind wir an der Grenze Belgiens. Hier liegt Sonne über Flächen, die mit Weinreben bepflanzt sind. Doch Ostende und Virton sind kaum 300 km voneinander entfernt.

Zwei große schiffbare Flüsse, die Schelde und die Maas, fließen von Süden nach Norden durch das Land. Schon zwei Jahrtausende lang fungieren sie als Bindeglieder zwischen den Anwohnern, sie schufen Gemeinsamkeiten und ermöglichten großen kulturellen Strömungen ihr weiteres Vordringen.

Die Schelde ist das Paradebeispiel eines seewärtigen Flusses. An ihren Ufern sammelten die Merowinger ihre Kräfte, bevor sie nach Paris vorstießen. In der Blütezeit der romanischen Kunst vollzog sich der Austausch in umgekehrter Richtung und der Einfluss kam vor allem aus Frankreich. In Tournai und Soignies entstanden die zum großen Teil an Leitbildern aus der Normandie orientierten religiösen Bauten, die für das Stromgebiet der Schelde maßgebend wurden. Sehr bald erhoben sich auch in der flandrischen Ebene und in Brabant, hauptsächlich in Gent und Brügge, Kirchen bauten, die sich an der Kathedrale von Tournai orientieren. Typische Baumerkmale kennzeichnen ebenfalls die gotischen Kirchen des Scheldebeckens, wobei die eigenartigen Züge die größere Aufgeschlossenheit gegenüber Einwirkungen aus dem Maasland nicht im Geringsten beeinträchtigten. Hinzu kommt natürlich auch, dass Antwerpen der Schelde seine Entwicklung als Hafenstadt verdankt.

Die Maas ist über weite Strecken hin waldumsäumt. In ihrem Stromgebiet bauten die Karolinger ihre Vormachtstellung aus, während sie an die Stelle der Merowinger traten und unter Karl dem Großen die Grenzen der Christenheit bis an die Ufer der Elbe verschoben. Daraus ergab sich in der Folgezeit ein Überwiegen germanischer Einflüsse. Notker, der eigentliche Gründer und große Fürstbischof Lüttichs, war ein von Otto I. ernannter Schwabe. Es braucht uns also nicht zu verwundern, dass z. B. die Johanneskirche nach dem Grundriss des achteckigen Aachener Doms gebaut wurde. Dies war der Anfang eines jahrhundertelangen kulturellen Austauschs innerhalb des Rhein-Maas-Gebiets.

Die wechselseitigen Beziehungen zwischen Schelde und Maas wurden seit dem Altertum entscheidend durch die in ostwestlicher Richtung verlaufende Heeresstraße gefördert, die Köln mit Boulogne, später mit Brügge verband. So wurde Brügge zum Handelszentrum, in dem Kaufleute die Erzeugnisse der eingesessenen Leinweber gegen Wolle aus England und Spanien oder Gewürze und andere Waren aus dem Orient eintauschten.

Die durch die Bevölkerungsdichte — 327 Einwohner pro Quadratkilometer — mitbedingte Verstädterung hat Belgien mehr als jedes andere Land geprägt. Jede Stadt hat ihre eigenen, auf ihre Enstehungsgeschichte oder vergangene Rivalitätskämpfe zurückzuführenden Wesensmerkmale, doch dasselbe Ringen um Freiheit und Selbstverwaltungsrecht verbindet seit langem vor allem die größeren Städte miteinander.

Die geographische Lage der belgischen Herzogtümer und Grafschaften, das wirtschaftliche Wachstum der Städte sowie Interessengemeinschaft führten unvermeidlich zu einander ablösenden Bündnissen, sozusagen einem Vorspiel zum «föderalen» Zusammenschluss unter den Herzögen von Burgund (aus dem Hause Valois), ganz besonders unter dem «Conditor Belgii» (= Gründer Belgiens) Philipp dem Guten (1419-1467). Wie um die Festigkeit dieser dynastisch gestifteten Bande unter Beweis zu stellen, beschenkten und bereicherten die Maler, Bildhauer, Musiker und Schriftsteller dieses «goldenen Jahrhunderts» Europa mit Werken, in denen eine gemeinsame Gesinnung und eine eigenartige, bodenständige Kultur zum Ausdruck gelangt. Es genüge, die Namen der Gebrüder Van Eyck, Rogier van der Weydens, Hans Memlings zu nennen.

Nachdem Maria von Burgund, die einzige Tochter des 1477 vor Nancy verschollenen Herzogs Karl des Kühnen (1500-1555), Maximilian von Österreich geheiratet hatte, kamen die Habsburger in den Niederlanden zum Zuge. Die Folge war eine Europäisierung, die zuerst glanzvoll zu werden versprach. Unter Karl V., der jede fremde Einmischung in den XVII Provinzen unterbunden hatte, blieb das Land das reichste Westeuropas. Antwerpen war eine Stadt, in der sich nicht nur Tausende Kaufleute und Bankiers, sondern auch Künstler und Gelehrte trafen und wurde nicht zu Unrecht als die Metropole der westlichen Welt bezeichnet.

Das beharrliche Bestehen auf heute selbstverständlichen Rechten — u. a. dem Recht auf Glaubensfreiheit — führte zum Aufstand gegen die Herrschsucht und die Unduldsamkeit Philipps II. und zur Spaltung der XVII Provinzen in zwei Teile: die kalvinistischen Vereinigten Provinzen im Norden (die heutigen Niederlande) und die katholischen Niederlande im Süden (heute Belgien und Luxemburg). In den südlichen Niederlanden lösten danach ausländische Herrscher und Besatzungstruppen einander ab, doch während dieser von kurzen Perioden wirtschaftlichen Auflebens unterbrochenen Jahrhunderte der Kriegswirren und Erniedrigung wuchsen die verschiedenen Landesteile auch enger zusammen. Die Quellen künstlerischer Bewältigung und literarischen Schaffens hörten übrigens auch nicht auf zu sprudeln : Brueghel und Patinir im 16., Rubens, Van Dijck und Jordaens im 17., der Fürst de Ligne und Grétry im 18. Jh. beweisen das zur Genüge.

Die anfangs eigentlich ungewollte Spaltung der XVII Provinzen zog im Laufe der Zeit eine Auseinanderentwicklung der Denkart im Norden und im Süden nach sich, die durch religiöse Unterschiede und wirtschaftliche Interessenkollisionen geschürt wurde. Die Nichtberücksichtigung dieser Tatsache seitens der Besieger Napoleons führte auf dem Wiener Kongreß (1814-1815) zu der Fehlentscheidung, Belgier und Holländer im Königreich der Niederlande vereinen zu wollen. Diese durch Zwang zustande gekommene Heirat bot zwar wirtschaftliche Vorteile, doch sie scheiterte schließlich an der Unverträglichkeit der Partner und am Mangel an Geschicklichkeit Wilhelms I. Fünfzehn Jahre später ließ die siegreiche Revolution von 1830 die Belgier nach jahrhundertelangem Warten das Ziel ihrer Träume erreichen. Sie bildeten einen unabhängigen Staat und wählten die verfassungsmäßige, parlamentarische Monarchie als Staatsform.

Die ersten belgischen Historiker versäumten kaum eine Gelegenheit, denen ins Gewissen zu reden, die den neuen Staat im Ausland als ein rein vertragsmäßiges Gebilde abtaten. J.-B. Nothomb, einer der begabtesten — er war zugleich Politiker und Diplomat —, schrieb 1833 in seinem «Historischen und politischen Essay über die belgische Revolution»: «Wenn sich Belgien seit zwei Jahrhunderten ununterbrochen in der Obhut anderer Völker befunden hat, geschah dies, weil es keine andere Wahl hatte. Die Tatsache, dass es unter den sich ablösenden ausländischen Mächten seinem eigenen Volkscharakter treu geblieben ist, beweist das. Es ist weder den Spaniern gelungen, die Belgier zu hispanisieren, noch den Österreichern, sie in Österreicher, noch den Holländern, sie in Holländer zu verwandeln. Im 16. Jh. erhoben sie sich gegen Spanien, im 18. gegen Österreich, im 19. gegen Holland. Wenn dieses Volk, wie behauptet wird, kein es begründendes Lebensprinzip in sich trägt, wie hat es dann so viele Mißgeschicke überstehen können? Falls es kein Nationalbewusstsein hat, warum hat es sich dann nicht in eine andere Nation eingegliedert? Es hat Frankreichs Anspruch zurückgewiesen, das es nur zwanzig Jahre zu besetzen vermochte. Vor Napoleon hat es sich in Schweigen gehüllt wie vor Ludwig XIV. und hat gewartet, bis sie vorbeigezogen waren. Alle Fahnen, gleißende und von jahrhundertealtem Ruhm umhüllte, hat man vor diesem Volk entrollt, es hat keiner zugejubelt, es hat sich seine eigene geschaffen. »

Nachdem ihn der nationale Kongress zum König erwählt hatte, beschränkte sich Leopold von Sachsen-Coburg-Gotha (1831-1865) nicht darauf, die internationale Stellung des belgischen Staates zu festigen; sein «kombinierender Geist», wie Metternich sagte, machte ihn zum Schiedsrichter im damaligen Europa.

Unter der Regierung Leopolds II. (1865-1909) gelang es Belgien, bis zum vierten Platz in der Weltrangliste der Handelsmächte aufzusteigen. Da ihm das Land nicht groß genug schien, um den wirtschaftlichen Schaffensdrang seiner Bevölkerung zu befriedigen, erteilte er dieser den Auftrag, das Herz Afrikas gegen die Sklavenhändler zu verteidigen und dessen Bodenschätze nutzbar zu machen. Der Kongo blieb eine belgische Kolonie bis ins Jahr 1960, als ihm Belgien aus freien Stücken die Unabhängigkeit verlieh.

Das «exponierteste Land der Welt» wurde von beiden Weltkriegen in Mitleidenschaft gezogen. 1914 nahm die belgische Wehrmacht unter Albert I., 1940 unter Leopold III. ihre Pflicht auf sich und kam all ihren aus internationalen Verträgen hervorgehenden Verpflichtungen nach.

Nach dem 2. Weltkrieg vollzog das Land unter König Baudouin nicht ohne Reibungen und Schwierigkeiten den Übergang zu einer föderativen Regierungsform, die den drei Gemeinschaften — der flämischen, der französisch- und der deutschsprachigen — sowie den drei Regionen — Flandern, der Wallonie und Brüssel-Hauptstadt — weitgehend die Selbstverwaltung der ihnen von der geänderten Verfassung zuerkannten Ressorts gewährt. Das von der französischen Besatzung herrührende Modell des zentralisierten Einheitsstaates wurde durch ein der Wirklichkeit und dem kulturellen Pluralismus des Staates besser angepasstes ersetzt. Wie König Balduin am 21. Juli 1993 in seinem politischen Testament ausführte, sind diese neuen, oft komplexen Strukturen nur dann lebensfähig, wenn sie von «föderalem Staatsbewusstsein» getragen werden. Auf diesen Zusammenhang wies auch Albert II. am 9. August 1993 in seiner Antrittsrede als sechster König Belgiens hin.

Zugleich spielte das Land auch außenpolitisch eine aktive Rolle. Es schloss sich mit den anderen Beneluxstaaten zu einer Wirtschaftsunion zusammen, wurde Mitbegründer der Vereinten Nationen sowie der von ihr abhängigen Hilfs- und Sonderorganisationen und Mitglied der NATO, deren Hauptquartier sich seit dem Ausscheiden Frankreichs in Belgien befindet. Es ist ferner eins der sechs Länder, die zusammen die Montanunion gründeten, und eins der Länder, die 1957 in Rom die Europäische Gemeinschaft ins Leben riefen. So ist Brüssel zur Zeit die faktische, wenngleich noch nicht die rechtlich anerkannte Hauptstadt der Europäischen Gemeinschaft, die mittels der Maastrichter Verträge auf dem Weg zur Einigung fortzuschreiten bestrebt ist.

◁

Succédant au marché aux poissons encore actif au XVIe siècle, le **marché aux herbes** donna son nom à la rue qui constitue une section de l'ancienne chaussée descendant du Coudenberg vers la Grand-Place. Aux XVIIe et XVIIIe siècles, ses nombreux magasins de luxe étaient fréquentés par la clientèle riche de la capitale.

De in de 16de eeuw nog druk bezochte vismarkt werd later door een **grasmarkt** vervangen, hetgeen de huidige naam van dit gedeelte van de straat verklaart, die de Coudenberg met de Grote Markt verbindt. In de 17de en 18de eeuw waren hier vooral luxezaken voor de welgestelde burgers.

Replacing the fish market which was still active in the 16th century, the **herb market** gave its name to the street forming part of the old road descending from the Coudenberg to the Grand-Place. In the 17th and 18th centuries its many luxury shops were patronized by the carriage trade of the capital.

Nachdem der im 16. Jh. noch dort florierende Fischmarkt einem **Kräutermarkt** das Feld überlassen hatte, erhielt dieser Teil der Straße, die den Coudenberg mit dem Marktplatz verband, seinen heutigen Namen. Im 17. und 18. Jh. befanden sich an jener Stelle vor allem teure Geschäfte für die vornehme Kundschaft.

▷

Les Bruxellois sont très attachés au **Manneken-Pis** que Jérôme Duquesnoy sculpta en 1619. Ils considèrent cette statuette de bronze — elle mesure à peine soixante centimètres — comme un talisman. La garde-robe complète du «plus ancien citoyen de Bruxelles», quelque deux cent soixante-cinq costumes, est conservée dans une salle de la *Maison du Roi*.

De Brusselaars houden bijzonder veel van **Manneken-Pis**, die in 1619 door Hiëronymus Duquesnoy werd gebeeldhouwd. Ze koesteren dit bronzen beeldje van amper 60 cm hoogte als een talisman. De kleerkast van de «oudste burger van Brussel» wordt bewaard in één der zalen van het *Broodhuis*. Zij bevat 265 klederdrachten.

The natives of Brussels are very fond of their **Manneken-Pis** sculpted by Jerome Duquesnoy in 1619. The statue is only 60 cm high but is a mascot for the people of Brussels. The wardrobe of this «oldest of Brussels' citizens», consisting of some 265 costumes, is kept in one of the halls of the King's House.

Die Einwohner Brüssels haben dem 1619 von Jérôme Duquesnoy gegossenen **Manneken-Pis** ihr Herz geschenkt. Für sie ist diese kleine, kaum 60 cm hohe Bronzestatue ein Talisman. Die vollständige Garderobe des «ältesten Bürgers von Brüssel», umfasst nicht weniger als 265 Trachten, die in einem Saal des *Hauses des Königs* aufbewahrt werden.

△
À **Bruxelles**, le **Mont des Arts** a remplacé un jardin romantique. Ses escaliers descendent vers la ville basse d'où surgit la tour de l'hôtel de ville. Dans le lointain se profile la puissante silhouette de la basilique du Sacré-Cœur achevée en 1969.

In **Brussel**, waar vroeger een romantische tuin lag, staat nu de **Kunstberg**. Trappen leiden naar het lager stadsgedeelte van waaruit de stadhuistoren oprijst. Aan de einder duiken de stoere contouren op van de Heilig-Hart-Basiliek, die in 1969 werd voltooid.

The present *Mont des Arts* in **Brussels** has taken the place of the romantic gardens that formerly occupied this site. The steps lead to the lower part of the city, dominated by the tower of the City Hall. In the distance is the powerful outline of the Basilica of the Sacred Heart, which was completed in 1969.

In **Brüssel** nimmt der **Kunstberg** den Platz eines früheren romantischen Gartens ein. Seine Treppen führen zur Unterstadt hinunter, aus der der Rathausturm hervorragt und hinter der sich in der Ferne der eindrucksvolle Umriss der 1969 vollendeten Herz-Jesu-Basilika abzeichnet.

▷
À Bruxelles, sur la côte sablonneuse jadis occupée par un oratoire de style roman, la construction d'une basilique nouvelle fut entreprise vers 1226. Elle se poursuivit jusqu'à la fin du XVᵉ siècle. La robuste sobriété du gothique brabançon triomphe dans les tours jumelles de la **cathédrale Saint-Michel**.

In Brussel, op de zanderige helling waarop een Romaanse kapel had gestaan, werd in 1226 met de bouw van een nieuwe basiliek gestart. De bouwwerkzaamheden duurden tot einde 15de eeuw. Beide torens van de **St-Michielskathedraal** zijn een zuiver voorbeeld van de gedegen soberheid der Brabantse gotiek.

Towards the year 1226 work began in Brussels on a new basilica, on the sandy slope where a Romanesque oratory used to stand. Work on the new building continued until the end of the 15th century. The twin towers of the **Cathedral of St. Michael** personify the sturdy sobriety of the Brabant Gothic style.

Der Bau der Kathedrale von Brüssel auf dem sandigen Abhang, auf dem früher ein Oratorium in romanischem Stil gestanden hatte, wurde 1226 in Angriff genommen. Er zog sich bis zum Ende des 15. Jh. hin. Die robuste Schmucklosigkeit des brabantisch-gotischen Stils triumphiert in den Zwillingstürmen der **St. Michaelskathedrale**.

△

La façade du **Palais de Charles de Lorraine** (1766) reprend, dans le style Louis XVI autrichien, les thèmes antiques avec une exquise élégance. Actuellement, il est au centre du quartier des arts groupant Palais des congrès, Musées royaux, Bibliothèque royale et Palais des Beaux-Arts.

Thema's uit de Oudheid verfraaien de vele bas-reliëfs en beelden van de gevel van het **Paleis van Karel van Lotharingen** in Oostenrijkse Lodewijk-XVI-stijl (1766). Het paleis vormt nu het hart van de kunstwijk, met verder nog het Congressenpaleis, de Koninklijke Musea, de Koninklijke Bibliotheek en het Paleis voor Schone Kunsten.

The facade of the **Palace of Charles of Lorraine** (1766) is an exquisite rendering of subjects from classical antiquity in the elegant Austrian Louis XVI style of 18th century architecture. Today, the building rises in the heart of the arts district which also comprises the Convention Center, the Royal Museums, the Royal Library and the Palace of Fine Arts.

Die Fassade des im österreichischen Louis XVI-Stil erbauten **Palais Karls von Lothringen** (1766) zeigt antiken Themen nachempfundene Flachreliefs und Statuen von ausgesuchter Formschönheit. Heute befindet er sich inmitten des sogenannten «Kunstviertels», welches den Kongresspalast, die Königlichen Museen, die Königliche Bibliothek und das Palais der Schönen Künste umfasst.

▷

Estimant l'ancien palais, que le roi Guillaume Ier des Pays-Bas avait conçu à partir de deux ailes du XVIIIe siècle, indigne du prestige de la monarchie, Léopold II entreprit dès 1867 des travaux d'agrandissement et de transformation. En 1904, une toute nouvelle façade fut édifiée dans le style Louis XVI. L'avant-corps central du **palais royal**, à double colonnade et fronton, est surmonté d'un dôme où flotte le drapeau national quand le roi est à Bruxelles.

Leopold II achtte het oude paleis, gebouwd door koning Willem I der Nederlanden en gebaseerd op twee vleugels uit de 18de eeuw, beneden de waardigheid van de monarchie. Daarom gaf hij opdracht om vanaf 1867 van start te gaan met uitbreidings- en veranderingswerken. In 1904 werd een volledig nieuwe gevel in Lodewijk XVI-stijl opgetrokken. Bovenop het centrale voorgebouw van het **koninklijk paleis**, met dubbele zuilenrij en fronton, staat een koepel. Telkens de koning in Brussel aanwezig is, wappert hierop de nationale driekleur.

Leopold II considered the old palace cobbled together from two 18th century buildings by King William I of the Netherlands as not fitting for his monarchy and thus began work to enlarge and remodel it in 1867. In 1904 a completely new façade in the Louis XVI Style was built. The central portion of the **Royal Palace** with the pediment and double colonnade is crowned with a dome where the national flag flies when the King is in residence.

Leopold II., der den alten Palast, den Wilhelm I. der Niederlande ausgehend von zwei Flügeln des 18. Jahrhunderts hatte errichten lassen, für das Prestige der Monarchie als unzureichend betrachtete, ließ ab 1867 Arbeiten zur Vergrößerung und Umgestaltung des Palastes durchführen. Im Jahre 1904 wurde eine neue Fassade im Louis-seize realisiert. Der in der Mitte befindliche Vorbau des **Königlichen Palastes**, der eine doppelte Säulenreihe und einen Giebel aufweist, wird von einer Kuppel überragt, auf der die belgische Flagge weht, wenn sich der König in Brüssel aufhält.

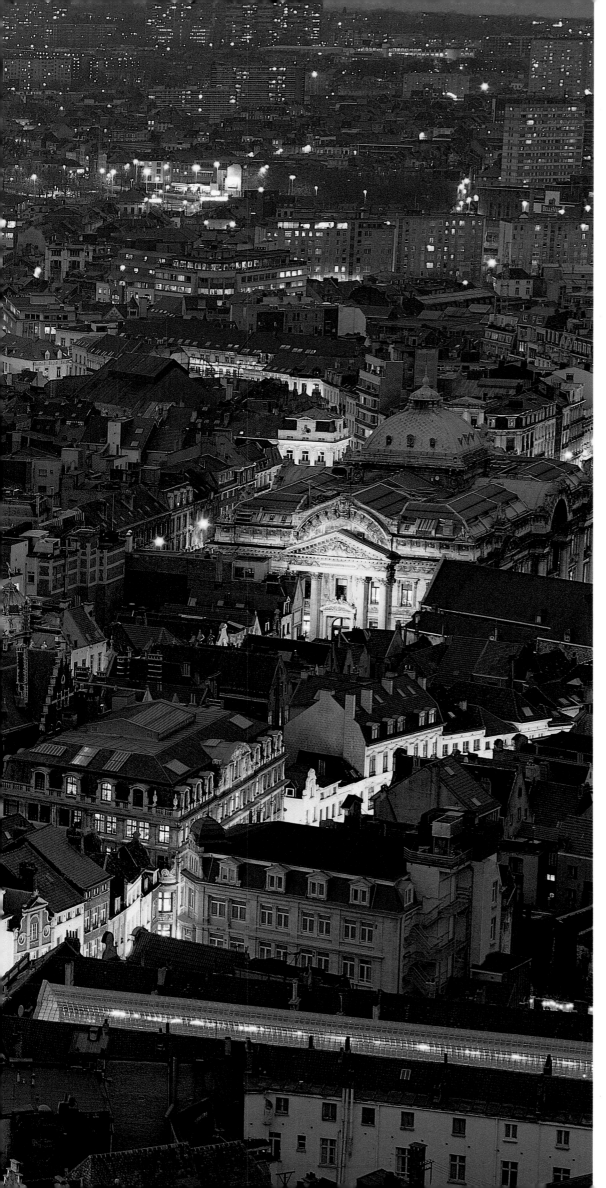

Voulant remplacer le beffroi, symbole des libertés communales, et couronner l'**hôtel de ville de Bruxelles**, le Magistrat fit appel en 1449 à Jan van Ruysbroeck. En cinq ans, le plus habile architecte de Philippe le Bon éleva une véritable dentelle de pierre qui surgit du sol d'un seul jet de nonante mètres de hauteur.

(Page suivante)

Incendié en 1695 lors du bombardement par l'artillerie française, l'intérieur de l'hôtel de ville de Bruxelles fut entièrement restauré. Les grandes salles mais aussi les différents cabinets de travail reçurent un décor nouveau. Le cabinet Renaissance doit son appellation à la monumentale cheminée de ce style.

In 1449 deed de Magistraat van Brussel een beroep op Jan van Ruysbroeck om het belfort, symbool van de gemeentelijke vrijheden, te vervangen en het **stadhuis van Brussel** te bekronen. De handigste architect van Filips de Goede bouwde in vijf jaar een waar kantwerk van steen dat in één stuk uit de grond oprees tot een hoogte van negentig meter.

(Volgende bladzijde)

Het stadhuis van Brussel werd in 1695 platgebrand door de bombardementen van de Franse artillerie. Het interieur werd dan ook volledig gerestaureerd. De grote zalen, maar ook verschillende werkkabinetten kregen een nieuwe inrichting. Het Renaissancekabinet dankt haar naam aan de monumentale schoorsteen in gelijknamige stijl.

When it was decided to replace the belfry, the symbol of municipal freedom, and to build a tower over the **Town Hall of Brussels** in 1449 the Mayor called in Jan van Ruysbroeck. In five years, Philip the Good's ablest architect built an edifice of stone lacework, rising to a height of almost 300 feet.

(Next page)

The interior of Brussels' City Hall, burned out in the 1695 bombardment by French artillery, was completely restored, both the large halls and various offices receiving a new decor. The Renaissance cabinet, lit by a large copper chandelier, derives its name from the monumental chimney-piece in that style.

Um den Bergfried, das Sinnbild der städtischen Freiheit, zu ersetzen und das **Rathaus von Brüssel** zu krönen, wandte sich der Magistrat 1449 an Jan van Ruysbroeck. In fünf Jahren errichtete der geschickteste Baumeister Herzog Philipps des Guten ein regelrechtes Spitzenwerk aus Stein, das sich in einem einzigen Wurf vom Boden bis zur Höhe von neunzig Metern emporschwingt.

(Nächste Seite)

Die Inneneinrichtung des Brüsseler Rathauses, das 1695 bei der Bombardierung durch die französische Artillerie in Flammen aufging, wurde vollständig restauriert. Die großen Säle wurden ebenso wie die einzelnen Arbeitszimmer mit einer neuen Einrichtung ausgestattet. Das Renaissancezimmer verdankt dem gewaltigen, in diesem Stil gestalteten Kamin seinen Namen.

(Pages 25 à 29)
La **Grand-Place de Bruxelles** occupe l'emplacement d'un marais asséché. Le marché de la ville s'y tenait dès le XIIe siècle. Son importance ne cessa de grandir sur les plans politique et économique. Par surcroît, elle servait de cadre aux tournois et aux Joyeuses Entrées des souverains. La reconstruction de ses maisons, après le bombardement français de 1695, se fit dans un style italo-flamand qui, malgré l'exubérance décorative, respectait les anciennes structures gothiques. Reconstruite en style néo-gothique, la *Maison du Roi* (1873-1895) s'apparente à un pastiche du XVIe siècle.

(Blz. 25 tot 29)
De **Grote Markt van Brussel** ontstond nadat het moeras er was drooggelegd. Reeds in de 12de eeuw werd er markt gehouden. Het plein speelde een steeds grotere rol op politiek en economisch vlak. Ter gelegenheid van toernooien en blijde inkomsten van vorsten schitterde het in alle pracht en praal. Na het bombardement door de Fransen in 1695 werden de huizen rond het plein in een Italiaans-Vlaamse stijl heropgebouwd die, alle siervormen ten spijt, de oude gotische bouwwijze indachtig bleef. Het veel later in neogotische bouwtrant gerestaureerde *Broodhuis* (1873-1895) lijkt op een pastiche van de 16de-eeuwse gebouwen.

(Pages 25 to 29)
The **Grand-Place of Brussels** stands on what was formerly a marsh, long since dried up. From the 12th century on the city market was held there and the square grew rapidly in political and economic importance. It also served as the site of tournaments and the *Joyeuses Entrées* of the rulers. Following the French bombardment of 1695 the houses surrounding the square where rebuilt in an Italo-Flemish style which, despite the exuberant decoration, respected the old Gothic forms. The neo-Gothic *Maison du Roi* built much later between 1873 and 1895 is a pastiche of the old 16th century style.

(S. 25 bis 29)
Der **Marktplatz von Brüssel** konnte erst entstehen, nachdem der dort befindliche Sumpf trockengelegt worden war. Bereits im 12. Jh. wurde an dieser Stelle Markt abgehalten. Seitdem stieg die politische und wirtschaftliche Bedeutung des Platzes fortwährend. Er gab Turnieren und fröhlichen Einzügen von Fürsten einen würdigen Rahmen. Nach der Bombardierung durch die Franzosen 1695 wurden die Häuser in italienisch-flämischem Stil wieder aufgebaut, wobei trotz der üppigen Ausschmückung die alten gotischen Strukturen beibehalten wurden. Die in neogotischem Stil restaurierte, auch «Haus des Königs» genannte Brothalle (1873-1895) ist Bauten des 16. Jh. nachgebildet.

▽
Lorsqu'en 1586 Charles de Gavre entreprit d'édifier le nouveau **château de Rixensart**, il le voulut de plan médiéval par la disposition des quatre ailes autour d'une cour centrale. Les travaux poursuivis entre 1648 et 1662 en accentuèrent le caractère de manoir de plaisance. Au style Renaissance appartiennent les trois galeries de la cour intérieure.

Toen Charles de Gavre in 1586 besloot het nieuwe **kasteel van Rixensart** te bouwen, wilde hij dit doen volgens een middeleeuwse plattegrond, met vier gebouwen rondom een centrale binnenkoer. De werken werden verdergezet tussen 1648 en 1662 en benadrukten het karakter van een lusthof. De renaissancestijl komt tot uiting in de drie galerijen van de binnenkoer.

Charles de Gavre wished to follow the mediæval plan of four wings around a central courtyard when he began building the new **castle of Rixensart** in 1586. Work done later from 1648 to 1662 put emphasis on its role as a country house. The three galleries of the inner courtyard are in the Renaissance style.

Als Charles de Gavre im Jahre 1586 mit dem Bau des neuen **Schlosses von Rixensart** begann, wollte er es in mittelalterlichem Stil errichten, wobei sich vier Flügel um einen Haupthof gruppieren sollten. Die Arbeiten, die zwischen 1648 und 1662 durchgeführt wurden, betonen den Lustschloss-Charakter. Im Renaissancestil sind die drei Galerien des Innenhofes gestaltet.

▷
Sur le plateau de Mont-Saint-Jean, la **butte du Lion** a été élevée à l'endroit où fut blessé le prince d'Orange, qui avait sous ses ordres les Belges et les Hollandais à la Bataille de Waterloo, le 18 juin 1815, qui provoqua la chute de Napoléon. Le lion de fonte qui domine la butte regarde la France.

Op het plateau van de Mont-Saint-Jean, op de plaats waar de aanvoerder van de Belgen en de Hollanders, de Prins van Oranje, werd gekwetst tijdens de slag om Waterloo, werd de **Leeuwenheuvel** opgericht. De avond van 18 juni 1815 vluchtte Napoleon naar Parijs. Boven de heuvel staat een bronzen leeuw met de blik naar Frankrijk gericht.

The **Lion's Mount** was erected on the plateau of Mont-Saint-Jean, at the spot where the Prince of Orange had been wounded in the Battle of Waterloo. It was he who had the Belgian and Dutch troops under his command. In the evening of 18 June, 1815 Napoleon fled to Paris. The cast iron lion at the top faces France.

Auf der Hochebene von Mont-Saint-Jean wurde der **Löwenhügel** an der Stelle errichtet, wo der Prinz von Oranien, unter dessen Befehl die Belgier und Holländer standen, verwundet wurde. Am Abend des 18. Juni 1815 desselben Tages flüchtete Napoleon nach Paris. Der Tag hatte 40.000 Franzosen und 22.000 Verbündeten das Leben gekostet. Der gusseiserne Löwe, der auf dem Hügel steht, blickt nach Frankreich.

Le Brabant wallon est séparé du Brabant flamand, près de Bruxelles, par la forêt de Soignes. Au sud de celle-ci, le relief s'accentue au gré de nombreux ruisseaux et rivières qui sillonnent le «roman pays». Sur les bords de leurs rives ou sur la pente de collines, les villages résidentiels se succèdent. À **Ohain**, depuis la place Communale qui s'apparente à un parc agrémenté d'une fontaine et d'un kiosque, on a vue sur la tour et la flèche de l'église du XVIᵉ siècle.

Vlakbij Brussel worden Waals-Brabant en Vlaams-Brabant van elkaar gescheiden door het Zoniënwoud. Ten zuiden hiervan wordt het reliëf bepaald door de grillen van de talloze stroompjes en riviertjes die het Romaanse land doorkruisen. Aan hun oevers of op de heuvelflanken volgen de dorpjes elkaar op. In **Ohain** heeft men vanaf het gemeenteplein, dat meer weg heeft van een park met fontein en kiosk, een zicht op de toren en de spits van de 16de-eeuwse kerk.

Walloon Brabant and Flemish Brabant are separated near Brussels by the Soignes forest. South of this the terrain is cut by numerous brooks and streams which flow through the "Roman country". Dormitory villages lie along their banks or on the hill slopes. From the town square in **Ohain**, resembling a park with a fountain and a kiosk, there is a fine view of the tower and steeple of the 16th century church.

Das wallonische Brabant wird in der Nähe von Brüssel durch den Soignes-Wald vom flämischen Brabant getrennt. In dessen Süden wird das Relief durch zahlreiche Bäche und Flüsse geprägt, die das "romanische Land" durchziehen. An den Flussufern und auf den Hängen der Hügel folgt eine Ortschaft auf die nächste. In **Ohain** eröffnet sich dem Besucher vom Dorfplatz aus, an den sich ein mit einem Brunnen und einem Pavillon geschmückter Park anschließt, ein Blick auf den Kirchturm und dessen Spitze aus dem 16. Jahrhundert.

△

Avec Braine-le-Château et Bois-Seigneur-Isaac, **Haut-Ittre** formait jadis un redan du comté de Hainaut dans le duché de Brabant. Bordée de petites fermes, la rue principale de ce village désormais brabançon-wallon monte vers l'église qui a gardé sa tour romane en grès du XIIe siècle.

Samen met Kasteelbrakel en Bois-Seigneur-Isaac vormde **Haut-Ittre** vroeger een insnijding van het graafschap Henegouwen in het hertogdom Brabant. Langs de hoofdstraat van dit nu Waals-Brabantse dorp liggen kleine boerderijen en rijst de dorpskerk op met haar zandsteentoren, die uit de 12de eeuw dateert.

Along with Braine-le-Château and Bois-Seigneur-Isaac, **Haut-Ittre** formed an outpost of the County of Hainaut in the Duchy of Brabant. The main street of the village, now part of Brabant Wallonia, is bordered by little farms and leads to the church which has retained its 12th century Romanesque tower.

Mit Braine-le-Château und Bois-Seigneur-Isaac bildete **Haut-Ittre** einen ins Herzogtum Brabant hineinragenden Zipfel der Grafschaft Hennegau. Die von kleinen Bauernhöfen umsäumte Hauptstraße des jetzt zum wallonischen Teil Brabants gehörenden Dorfes steigt bis zur Kirche hin an, deren romanischer Turm aus Sandstein aus dem 12. Jh. stammt.

▷

Trois quarts de siècle (1200 à 1272) furent consacrés à l'édification des trois nefs de l'église abbatiale de **Villers-la-Ville**. Quelques heures suffirent aux révolutionnaires français pour les détruire. Les intempéries firent le reste, provoquant en 1874 l'effondrement des voûtes. Les ruines révèlent encore le style champenois de l'édifice où, jusqu'à la fin du XVIIIe siècle, quelque quatre cents moines et convers se réunissaient pour la prière.

De bouw van de drie beuken van de abdijkerk van **Villers-la-Ville** had meer dan 70 jaar in beslag genomen (1200-1272), maar de Franse revolutionairen hadden slechts enkele uren nodig om ze te vernielen. De aan weer en wind blootgestelde gewelven stortten in 1874 in, maar de ruïnes laten nog de uit de Champagne stammende bouwstijl vermoeden van de abdij, die tot laat in de 18de eeuw 400 monniken en lekenbroeders telde.

Nearly three quarters of a century (1200 to 1272) were required to build the three naves of the abbey church of **Villers-la-Ville** but only a few hours were required by French revolutionary troops to destroy it. Weather accomplished the rest, causing the collapse of the vaulting in 1874. The ruins reveal the influence of the Champagne regional style on the building in which some 400 monks and lay brothers met in prayer until the end of the 18th century.

Während der Bau der dreischiffigen Abteikirche von **Villers-la-Ville** drei Vierteljahrhunderte gedauert hatte (1200-1272), benötigten die französischen Revolutionäre nur einige Stunden, um sie zu zerstören. Die Unbilden des Wetters verschlimmerten die Lage, so dass die Gewölbe 1874 einstürzten. Doch die Ruinen lassen noch den aus der Champagne kommenden Stil des Gotteshauses erahnen, in dem sich bis zum Ende des 18. Jh. etwa 400 Mönche und Brüder zum Gebet versammelten.

◁

Hof te Wedem met zijn vierkante toren, het aanleunende torentje en de in polygonale vorm geplaatste woongebouwen is een typisch Brabantse hoeve vlak bij Halle. Het witgekalkte hoofdgebouw uit de 17de eeuw, evenals de bedrijfsgebouwen uit de 19de eeuw, omsluiten een geplaveide binnenkoer.

La tour carrée accolée d'une tourelle et le polygone des bâtiments font de la **ferme de Wedem** un bel exemple de ferme brabançonne sur les terres de Hal. Blanchis à la chaux, le corps de logis qui est du XVIIᵉ siècle et les constructions du XIXᵉ forment un ensemble clos autour d'une cour pavée.

A fine example of a Brabant farm in the region of Hal is the **Hof te Wedem** with its square tower and turret and buildings forming a polygonal. The whitewashed main building is 17th century while 19th century additions surround the paved courtyord.

Die um den viereckigen Turm mit angebauten Türmchen errichteten Gebäude verleihen **Hof te Wedem** die Form eines Vielecks. Es ist ein typischer Brabanter Bauernhof in der Nähe von Halle. Das mit Kalk geweißte Hauptgebäude aus dem 17. sowie die Wirtschaftsgebäude aus dem 19. Jh. umschließen den gepflasterten Hof von allen Seiten.

△

Het enkele hectaren grote parkgedeelte van het Provinciaal Domein **Huizingen** bevat prachtige perken waarop de azalea's in de lente de symbolische betekenis van de kleuren tentoonspreiden: geel voor roem, groen voor hoop, rood voor hartstocht en paars als zinspeling op liefdesavontuurtjes.

Le vaste domaine provincial de **Huizingen** comporte plusieurs hectares de jardins. Aux jours de printemps, les variétés d'azalées y déploient généreusement les nuances de leurs couleurs dont la tradition rapporte la symbolique: le jaune de la gloire, le vert de l'espérance, le rouge de l'ardeur ou le violet de la galanterie.

The vast provincial domain of **Huizingen** has several hectares of gardens. In spring various varities of azaleas display their colours and traditional symbolism: yellow for glory, green for hope, red for courage and violet for gallantry.

Die Domäne der Provinz Brabant in **Huizingen** umfasst einige Hektar Gartenanlagen. Im Frühling breiten da Azalien verschiedenster Sorten einen Farbenteppich aus, der von Farbensymbolik strotzt: Gelb für den Ruhm, Grün für die Hoffnung, Rot für die Leidenschaft, Veilchenblau für galante Liebesabenteuer.

△

Op het binnenplein van het kasteel van **Gaasbeek** staat men voor de gevels van een fraai renaissancekasteel. Het machtige verdedigingsbolwerk van Gaasbeek was in 1388 verwoest door de Brusselse militie, die wraak nam voor de moord op Everard 't Serclaes. Nadat de Milanese markiezen Arconati-Visconti het kasteel even voor 1800 hadden geërfd, liet de laatste, nogal eigengereide nakomelinge van deze markiezen het in de 19de eeuw in romantische geest restaureren.

La cour intérieure du château de **Gaasbeek** révèle les façades d'une aimable demeure Renaissance. En 1388, le puissant appareil défensif de Gaasbeek n'évita pas un sac par les milices bruxelloises avides de venger le meurtre d'Everard 't Serclaes. À la fin du XVIIIᵉ siècle, il devint par héritage la propriété des marquis milanais Arconati-Visconti. La dernière et fantasque marquise fit restaurer le manoir à la manière romantique, chère au XIXᵉ siècle.

The inner courtyard of the castle of **Gaasbeek** is bordered with pleasant Renaissance facades. In 1388, despite its powerful defences, Gaasbeek was sacked by the Brussels militiamen intent on avenging the murder of Everard 't Serclaes. At the end of the 18th century it was inherited by the Milanese Marquis Arconati-Visconti. The last, unpredictable marchioness had the manor restored in the Romantic manner much in fashion in the 19th century.

Auf dem Innenhof des Schlosses von **Gaasbeek** steht der Besucher vor den Fassaden eines schmucken Renaissancehauses. Die wuchtige Burg von Gaasbeek war nämlich 1388 von Brüsseler Stadttruppen, die die Ermordung von Everard 't Serclaes rächen wollten, verwüstet worden. Nachdem es ein mailändischer Marquis Arconati-Visconti kurz vor 1800 geerbt hatte, ließ dessen letzter Nachfahre, eine recht eigenwillige Frau, das Schloss im 19. Jh. im damals üblichen romantischen Stil umgestalten.

▷

Het ten tijde van Karel de Stoute door Mattheus de Laeyens gebouwde **stadhuis van Leuven**, dat in 1447 werd begonnen en in 1460 werd voltooid, lijkt op een reusachtig relikwieschrijn waarvan de drie verdiepingen met telkens tien traveeën door uitspringende dwarslagen van elkaar zijn gescheiden.

Commencé en 1447 et terminé en 1460 sous le règne de Charles le Téméraire, l'**hôtel de ville de Louvain**, construit par Mathieu de Laeyens, ressemble à une châsse géante où dix travées de trois étages sont séparées entre elles par des trumeaux saillants.

Work on the **Town Hall of Louvain**, built by Mathieu de Laeyens, was begun in 1447 and completed in 1460, under the reign of Charles the Bold. It resembles a vast reliquary in which ten three storey spans are separated by jutting piers.

Das 1447 begonnene und 1460 während der Regierungszeit Karls des Kühnen vollendete **Rathaus der Stadt Löwen** wurde nach Plänen von Mathias de Laeyens errichtet. Es gleicht einem riesigen Reliquienschrein, dessen zehn, auf drei Stockwerke verteilte Felder horizontal durch hervortretende Gesims voneinander getrennt sind.

In **Tervuren**, waar het kasteel van de hertogen van Brabant zich verhief, woonplaats van de gulhartige Karel van Lotharingen en de ongelukkige Charlotte van Mexico, liet Leopold II een museum-paleis bouwen naar de plannen van de Franse architect Charles Girault.

De overkoepelde ronde hal in Lodewijk-XVI-stijl wijst op de zin voor het grandioze van de vorst.

It is at **Tervuren**, where the Dukes of Brabant had their castle and where the jovial Charles of Lorraine stayed, as well as the unhappy Empress Charlotte of Mexico, that Leopold II had a palace-cum-museum built, after plans of the French architect Charles Girault.

The Louis XVI style rotunda under the dome is an example of the grandiose taste of the monarch.

À **Tervueren**, où s'éleva le château des ducs de Brabant, où séjournèrent le jovial Charles de Lorraine et l'infortunée impératrice Charlotte du Mexique, Léopold II fit construire un palais-musée, suivant les plans de l'architecte français Charles Girault.

Sous la coupole, la rotonde de style Louis XVI témoigne du sens de la grandeur du souverain.

In **Tervuren**, wo sich das Schloss der Herzöge von Brabant erhob, in dem sich der joviale Karl von Lothringen und die unglückliche Kaiserin Charlotte von Mexiko aufhielten, ließ Leopold II. ein palastartiges Museum nach den Plänen des französischen Architekten Charles Girault erbauen.

Die von einer Kuppel überragte Rotunde im Louis-seize bezeugt den Sinn für Größe und die Vorliebe des Fürsten für stattliche Ausmaße.

◁

De inscriptie boven het barokke portaal (1671) van het **begijnhof te Diest** suggereert op meesterlijke wijze de sfeer die in dit besloten en stille toevluchtsoord heerst: « Besloten hof — Comt in mijnen hof, mijn suster, mijn bruyt. »

L'inscription sur le portail baroque (1671) du **béguinage de Diest** évoque à merveille l'atmosphère préservée de ce refuge du silence : « Jardin clos. Viens dans mon jardin clos, ma sœur, mon épousée. »

The legend on the baroque portal (1671) of the **Beguinage at Diest** evokes wonderfully the protective atmosphere of this quiet refuge : « Secret garden. Come into my secret garden, my sister, my wife. »

Die Inschrift über dem barocken Portal (1671) des **Klosters der Beginen in Diest** beschwört auf eindringliche Weise die wohlbehütete Welt dieses stillen Zufluchtsortes herauf : « Komme in meinen umfriedeten Garten, meine Schwester, meine Braut. »

▷

Onze-Lieve-Vrouw-ten-Poel in **Tienen** werd tussen 1200 en 1400 opgetrokken. De plannen van deze indrukwekkende gotische kerk met stevige steunberen en drie grootse portalen met boogtrommel worden aan de Franse bouwmeester Jean d'Oisy toegeschreven.

Imposant édifice gothique commencé au XIIIe siècle et terminé deux siècles plus tard, l'église Notre-Dame-au-Lac de **Tirlemont** présente, entre d'épais contreforts, trois portails monumentaux à voussures que l'on attribue à l'architecte français Jean d'Oisy.

The imposing Gothic church of Our Lady of the Lake at **Tienen** was begun in the 13th century and finished two centuries later. Between thick buttresses stand three monumental archivolted portals attributed to the French architect Jean d'Oisy.

Die prachtvolle gotische Kirche Unserer-Lieben-Frau-am-See in **Tienen** mit ihren wuchtigen Strebepfeilern und drei eindrucksvollen Portalen mit Bogenlaibung entstand hauptsächlich im 13. und 15. Jh. Der französische Baumeister Jean d'Oisy soll sie entworfen haben.

Volgens de legende hakte de reus Antigoon, die post had gevat op de oevers van de Schelde, de rechterhand af van de schippers die zijn tolrecht probeerden te omzeilen. Vervolgens gooide hij de bloederige hand van zijn slachtoffers in de golven, een gebaar — *hand werpen* — waaraan men lange tijd de oorsprong van de naam **Antwerpen** heeft toegekend. Op een dag ging Antigoon een gevecht van man tegen man aan met de listige Brabo. Het werd zijn ondergang : Brabo nam wraak op de verminkingen toegebracht aan talloze schippers en hakte zowel de rechter- als de linkerhand van de reus af. Om de herinnering aan deze legendarische daad levend te houden, heeft Jef Lambeaux voor het stadhuis van de metropool het standbeeld van Brabo opgericht op een voetstuk van rotsen, zeehonden en zeemeerminnen.

According to legend the giant Antigon who lurked on the banks of the Scheldt used to cut off the right hands of sailors who tried to avoid paying his tolls. He then threw the bloody hands of his victims into the waters. This deed — *hand werpen* — was long said to be the origin of the name of **Antwerp**. One day Antigon was engaged in single combat by the cunning Brabo. This was the giant's undoing: in revenge for the mutilated sailors Brabo cut off both the right and left hands of the giant. The statue of Brabo, standing on a socle of rocks, seals and sirens in front of the City Hall, was created by Jef Lambeaux to honor this legendary exploit.

Selon la légende, le géant Antigon, posté sur les rives de l'Escaut, tranchait le poignet droit des marins qui tentaient d'esquiver son droit de péage. Il jetait alors dans les flots la main sanglante de ses victimes, geste — *hand werpen* — auquel on attribua longtemps l'origine du nom **Antwerpen**. Un jour, Antigon affronta en combat singulier le rusé Brabo. Ce fut sa perte : vengeant les mutilations de nombreux marins, Brabo trancha la dextre et la sénestre du géant. Pour évoquer cet exploit légendaire, Jef Lambeaux a érigé devant l'hôtel de ville de la Métropole la statue ruisselante de Brabo sur un socle de rochers, de phoques et de sirènes.

Der Legende zufolge schlug der Riese Antigon, der an den Ufern der Schelde Posten bezogen hatte, Seeleuten, welche versuchten, ihm den geforderten Tribut zu verweigern, die rechte Hand ab. Die blutende Hand seiner Opfer warf er dann in die Fluten. Auf diesen Vorgang — *hand werpen* — wurde lange Zeit der Ursprung des Namens **Antwerpen** zurückgeführt. Eines Tages stand Antigon dem schlauen Brabo im Kampf gegenüber. Dies war seine Niederlage: Brabo rächte die Verstümmelung der zahlreichen Seeleute und schlug dem Riesen beide Hände ab. Zur Erinnerung an dieses legendäre Ereignis hat Jef Lambeaux vor dem Rathaus der Metropole die Statue von Brabo auf einem Sockel mit Felsen, Seehunden und Sirenen errichtet.

Op talrijke etsen uit de 16de eeuw staan stadsgezichten afgebeeld van **Antwerpen**, gezien van op de linkeroever van de Schelde. Niettegenstaande alle wijzigingen in het stadsbeeld, o.a. door de oprichting van het stoere, 87 m hoge Torengebouw (1929-1930), steekt de toren van de O.-L.-Vrouwekathedraal nog altijd boven de stad uit.

Le panorama d'**Anvers**, vu depuis la rive gauche de l'Escaut, a fréquemment inspiré les graveurs du XVIᵉ siècle. Il a considérablement changé depuis lors, mais la prestigieuse tour de Notre-Dame le domine toujours malgré la présence massive du *Torengebouw* (1929-1930), gratte-ciel qui atteint quatre-vingt-sept mètres.

The panorama of **Antwerp** seen from the left bank of the Scheldt often inspired 16th century engravers. It has changed considerably since then, but the renowned tower of Our Lady still stands out despite the massive Torengebouw (1929-1930) skyscraper which is 87 meters high.

Die vom linken Scheldeufer aus gesehene **Skyline Antwerpens** wurde im 16. Jh. wiederholt auf Kupferstichen abgebildet. Obschon sich inzwischen vieles verändert hat, überragt der großartige Turm der Liebfrauenkirche noch immer alles, sogar den 87 m hohen Wolkenkratzer, das 1929-1930 errichtete Torengebouw.

◁

De grote renaissancepoort van *El Valenciano*, Zirkstraat 34 te **Antwerpen**, verleent toegang tot een binnenplein. Het vrij indrukwekkende pand bevat o.a. een galerij uit de 17de eeuw. De afmetingen van de kelders laten vermoeden dat het ooit de zoutbeurs is geweest.

The huge Renaissance door of *El Valenciano* at 34 Zirkstraat in **Antwerp** opens onto the inner courtyard. A 17th century gallery forms part of this imposing building; the huge cellars may have been used formerly as the salt market.

La grande porte Renaissance d'*El Valenciano*, au 34 de la Zirkstraat à **Anvers**, s'ouvre sur la cour intérieure. Une galerie du XVIIᵉ siècle fait corps avec le bâtiment qui ne manque pas d'ampleur. Les vastes caves font d'ailleurs croire que le bâtiment servit jadis de bourse du sel.

Das im Renaissancestil gebaute Tor des *El Valenciano*, 34 Zirkstraße in **Antwerpen**, führt zum Innenhof des stattlichen Gebäudes, zu dem auch eine Galerie aus dem 17. Jh. gehört. Die Ausmaße der Kellerräume führen zur Annahme, dass an diesem Stapelplatz wahrscheinlich Salz gehandelt wurde.

△

In **Antwerpen** wordt het **Brouwershuis** (Adriaan de Brouwerstraat) ook „Waterhuis" genoemd, omdat Gilbert van Schoonbeek (1519-1556) er een waterinstallatie voor de drinkwatertoevoer naar de brouwerijen uit de buurt heeft laten bouwen. Van Schoonbeek was niet alleen een erg vooruitziend machinebouwer. Deze voorname handelaar en grondspeculant van het zuiverste water richtte de Nieuwstad op, waar het overbevolkte oud Antwerpen, met meer dan 100.000 inwoners, dringend nood aan had om verder te kunnen groeien.
De vergaderzaal is één van de mooiste 16de-eeuwse interieurs.

The **Brewer's House in Antwerp** in Adriaan de Brouwersstraat is also called "Hydraulic House" because Gilbert van Schoonbeek (1519-56) had it built to supply the neighbourhood breweries with fresh water. A daring engineer, businessman and real-estate speculator, Gilbert van Schoonbeek built a much-needed new town to expand and relieve Antwerp, overpopulated by its more than 100,000 inhabitants.
The meeting room is one of the most handsome remaining of the 16th century.

À **Anvers**, la **Maison des Brasseurs** (Adriaan de Brouwerstraat) est dite aussi «maison hydraulique» parce que Gilbert van Schoonbeek (1519-1556) la fit construire pour approvisionner en eau potable les brasseries du quartier. Ingénieur audacieux, grand commerçant et spéculateur immobilier, il ajouta au vieil Anvers qui souffrait de surpopulation — plus de cent mille habitants — la ville nouvelle dont elle avait besoin pour son expansion.
La salle des séances constitue l'un des plus beaux intérieurs du XVIᵉ siècle.

Das **Haus der Bierbrauer** in der Adriaan de Brouwerstraat in Antwerpen wird auch als das "hydraulische Haus" bezeichnet, da Gilbert van Schoonbeek (1519-1556) es zur Trinkwasserversorgung der im Viertel ansässigen Bierbrauer errichtet hatte. Als innovativer Ingenieur, Großkaufmann und Immobilienspekulant erweiterte er den alten Stadtkern von Antwerpen, in dem mehr als einhunderttausend Menschen dicht gedrängt zusammenlebten, um die Neustadt, die für die Stadtausdehnung dringend benötigt wurde.
Die Inneneinrichtung des Sitzungssaals ist eine der schönsten des 16. Jahrhunderts.

◁

De in 1899 verbrede en zeer drukke **Leysstraat** verbindt het Teniersplein met de nog drukkere Antwerpse Meir. De luxueuze gebouwen aan weerskanten munten qua stijl uit door prachtlievendheid en eenheid in verscheidenheid. Het paremenwerk van haast uitsluitend witte steen en de vrij eenvormige geledingen laten veel speelruimte aan het eclectisme dat typisch was voor de bouwkunst rond de eeuwwisseling (1895-1905) en er niet voor terugdeinsde neoclassicistische en neobarokke vormelementen naast elkaar te plaatsen. Deze straat, waarvan de naam aan de Antwerpse landschapsschilder Hendrik Leys (1815-1869) herinnert, werd terecht als voorbeeld van de eclectische monumentale architectuur geklasseerd en is dus in haar geheel beschermd.

La très commerçante **rue Leys**, élargie en 1899, joint la place Teniers au Meir d'Anvers. Les riches immeubles qui la bordent frappent d'abord par l'opulence et l'homogénéité. Mais l'unité n'empêche pas la diversité: malgré l'usage uniforme de la pierre blanche dans les parements et la régularité des nervures, l'éclectisme architectural à la mode au tournant des XIXe et XXe siècles permet la juxtaposition des styles néo-classique et néo-baroque. À juste titre, cette rue qui porte le nom du peintre anversois Henri Leys (1815-1869) a été classée comme paysage urbain et, comme telle, elle bénéficie de la protection de son ensemble.

The busy commercial **Leysstraat**, linking Teniers square to the Meir of Antwerp, was widened in 1899. The opulence and homogenity of the handsome buildings lining it is quite remarkable. However, unity does not prevent diversity. The architectural eclecticism in vogue at the turn of the 19th century allowed the juxtaposition of neo-classic and neo-baroque styles, which harmonize by means of the uniform use of white dressed stone and the regularity of the ribbing. This street, named after the Antwerp artist Henri Leys (1815-1869), has deservedly been classified as an urban landscape and, as such, is protected in its entirety.

Die 1899 verbreiterte **Leysstraat** ist eine Geschäftsstraße und verbindet das Teniersplein mit dem Meir in Antwerpen. Die Gebäude die Straße entlang zeugen von großem Wohlstand und sind zugleich aneinander angeglichen und doch sehr verschieden. Obschon fast überall weiße Steine als Mauerschmuck verwendet werden und es nicht an Übereinstimmungen in der Gliederung fehlt, schreckt der Eklektizismus der Jahrhundertwende (1895-1905) nicht vor der Konfrontation von neoklassizistischem und neubarockem Stilgut zurück. Nicht zu Unrecht wurde die Leysstraat, deren Namen an den Antwerpener Landschaftsmaler H. Leys (1815-1869) erinnert, als städtische Landschaft und Beispiel des Eklektizismus in der Baukunst unter Denkmalschutz gestellt und ist somit als Ganzes gesetzlich geschützt.

△

Het nieuwe **station van Antwerpen** werd in 1898 met veel luister ingehuldigd. Het gebouw, dat als twee druppels water op het station van Milaan lijkt, werd in 1905 afgewerkt en toont een gedurfde combinatie van een metalen structuur en een glazen overkapping. In de neo-barokke architectuur van de grote inkomhal is kwistig omgesprongen met marmer in verschillende kleuren. Op 60 meter hoogte boven de vloermozaïeken bevindt zich een koepel.

La nouvelle **gare d'Anvers** fut inaugurée avec éclat en 1898. Tout comme la gare de Milan qui lui ressemble d'une manière frappante, l'édifice terminé en 1905 réalise audacieusement le mariage d'une structure métallique et d'un bouclier de verre. L'architecture néo-baroque du grand hall utilise généreusement les marbres de différentes couleurs. Une coupole est posée à soixante mètres des mosaïques du sol.

The new **Antwerp railway station** was opened to great acclaim in 1898. The building which was finished in 1905, like the strikingly similar station in Milan, is an audacious marriage of a metal skeleton and glass cladding. Different colors of marble are lavishly employed in the neo-baroque hall. A cupola rises sixty meters above the mosaics of the floor.

Der neue **Antwerpener Bahnhof** wurde mit einer spektakulären Einweihungsfeier im Jahre 1898 eröffnet. Das Gebäude, das dem Mailänder Bahnhof verblüffend ähnelt, wurde 1905 fertiggestellt und vereint auf innovative Weise die Materialien Metall und Glas. Die große Halle in neobarockem Stil ist großflächig mit Mosaikstrukturen verschiedenster Farben ausgelegt, über denen sich in 60 Metern Höhe eine Glaskuppel erhebt.

51

De Fortuin te Lier dateert uit de 16de en 17de eeuw en was achtereenvolgens een opslagplaats voor graan, dan voor steenkool, vervolgens een limonadefabriek en een winkel. Het gebouw werd gerestaureerd en ingericht als restaurant, met zicht op de Nete. Een windwijzer in de vorm van Vrouwe Fortuna werd bovenop het dak geplaatst.

Successivement entrepôt de grains puis de charbon, fabrique de limonade et magasin de la ville, *De Fortuin* **à Lierre** date des XVIe et XVIIe siècles. Restauré, le bâtiment a été aménagé en restaurant ayant vue sur la Nèthe. Une girouette représentant Fortuna a été posée à son sommet.

Once a granary, then a coal storehouse, a soda factory and finally a town warehouse, **"De Fortuin"** in Lier dates from the 16th and 17th centuries. The building has been restored and converted into a restaurant overlooking the Nèthe. A weathervane representing Fortune stands on the roof.

"De Fortuin" in Lier, der nacheinander als Kornspeicher, Kohlespeicher, Limonadenfabrik und Stadtlager gedient hat, stammt aus dem 16. und 17. Jahrhundert. Bei der Restaurierung wurde das Gebäude in ein Restaurant mit Blick auf die Nete umgebaut. Auf der Spitze ist eine Wetterfahne zu sehen, die Fortuna darstellt.

Het voormalige **refugiehuis van de Benedictijnenabdij van Sint-Truiden** (1551-1611) in **Mechelen** staat aan de oever van één van de overblijfsels van de Melaan, een Mechels vlietje. De drie vleugels zijn een typisch voorbeeld van Vlaamse bouwkunst in rode baksteen en werden in 1920 gerestaureerd. De vijf verdiepingen van de fraaie achthoekige toren zijn telkens door een laag witte steen van elkaar gescheiden.

Le **refuge de l'abbaye bénédictine de Saint-Trond** (1551-1611) fut édifié au bord de la Melaan, qui traversait jadis **Malines** mais dont il ne reste qu'un bras mort. Ses trois ailes, typiques de l'architecture flamande en briques rouges, ont été restaurées en 1920. Quant à la fine tourelle octogonale, elle dresse gracieusement cinq registres séparés par des cordons en pierre blanche.

At the edge of a small lake, all that remains of the Melaan river that once flowed through **Mechelen**, stands the former **refuge of the Benedictine abbey of Sint-Truiden** (1551-1611). The three wings in the red brick typical of Flemish architecture were restored in 1920. A slender octagonal turret rises gracefully in five storeys, defined by white stone string courses.

Am Rand einer kleinen Wasserfläche, einem Überbleibsel des Melaans, eines der vielen früher durch Mechelen strömenden Bächlein, steht das **Refugium der Benediktinerabtei von Sint-Truiden** (1551-1611) in **Mechelen**. Die drei Flügel des Gebäudes sind aus dem für die flämische Baukunst typischen roten Backstein und wurden 1920 restauriert. Die fünf Stockwerke des schlanken, achteckigen Turms sind jeweils durch eine Zwischenschicht aus weißem Stein gekennzeichnet.

△

Alhoewel gedomineerd door de kloeke verticale toren van de St-Romboutskathedraal, kan de **Grote Markt van Mechelen** bogen op een indrukwekkende reeks huizen uit de 16de en 17de eeuw. Laatgotische trapgevels wisselen af met krulvormige die tijdens de bloeiperiode van de barok zijn ontstaan.

The imposing vertical tower of Saint Rombaut's cathedral overlooks the **main square in Mechelen**, which can be proud of its harmonious group of 16th and 17th century houses. The step-gables of some are late Gothic, while the voluted gables of others represent the baroque style in full bloom.

Dominée par la verticalité impérieuse de la tour de la cathédrale Saint-Rombaut, la **grand-place de Malines** peut s'enorgueillir d'un ensemble cohérent de maisons des XVIe et XVIIe siècles. Les pignons à redents des unes révèlent la fin du gothique tandis que les pignons à volutes des autres marquent l'épanouissement du style baroque.

Die vertikale Wucht des Turmes der St.-Rombautskathedrale wirft oft ihren mächtigen Schatten auf den **Marktplatz von Mecheln**, doch dieser kann stolz mit einer stattlichen und recht einheitlichen Reihe schöner Häuser aus dem 16. und 17. Jh. aufwarten. Während der ausgezahnte obere Giebelrand der einen auf das Ende der Gotik hinweist, künden die schwung vollen Spiralen der Giebelaufsätze anderer vom Siegeszug des Barockstils.

Het **Hof van Busleyden** werd in 1507 gebouwd in **Mechelen**. Het verenigt de overheersende laatgotische elementen met de eerste invloeden van de Renaissance : getuige hiervan is de dubbele galerij met arcades in rondboog die uitzien op de tuin. In 1619 werd het gebouw omgevormd tot Berg van Barmhartigheid waar de arme Mechelaars een renteloze lening konden aangaan. Het gebouw brandde af in 1915 en is nu, na een volledige restauratie tussen 1930 en 1938, het stadsmuseum.

Édifié à **Malines** en 1507, l'**hôtel de Busleyden** mêle aux éléments dominants du gothique tardif les premières influences de la Renaissance: en témoigne la double galerie qui dresse ses arcades en plein cintre devant le jardin. En 1619, l'édifice fut converti en Mont-de-Piété où les Malinois désargentés pouvaient emprunter sans intérêt. Incendié en 1915, il fut complètement restauré entre 1930 et 1938 et devint le musée communal.

The **Busleyden Mansion**, built in **Mechelen** in 1507, mixes early Renaissance elements with the dominant late Gothic architecture as in the double gallery supported by Roman arches in the garden. In 1619 the building became the municipal pawn shop where citizens short on funds could get interest-free loans. Victim of a fire in 1915 it was completely restored in 1930-38 and became the municipal museum.

Der **Busleydener Hof**, der 1507 in **Mecheln** erbaut wurde, weist neben den dominanten spätgotischen Elementen die ersten Renaissanceeinflüsse auf: Davon zeugt die doppelte Galerie, die ihre Rundbögenarkaden vor dem Garten zur Schau stellt. Im Jahre 1619 wurde das Gebäude in ein Pfandhaus umgewandelt, in dem sich die in Geldnöten geratenen Einwohner von Mechelen zinslos Geld leihen konnten. Das 1915 bei einem Feuer zerstörte Gebäude wurde zwischen 1930 und 1938 wieder aufgebaut und zum Stadtmuseum umfunktioniert.

De schiervlakte van **Haspengouw** strekt zich uit over de taalgrens. De streek dankt haar uitzonderlijke vruchtbaarheid aan het leem uit het Quartair tijdperk. Naast graangewassen en suikerhoudende planten, vindt men op de zachte glooiingen van de oostelijke zijde ook weides beplant met fruitbomen. In de lente worden de dorpen omringd door de bloesems van de boomgaarden. Die van **Kuttekoven** staan rondom de parochiekerk, die haar mooie Romaanse toren heeft behouden.

À cheval sur la «frontière linguistique», la pénéplaine de **Hesbaye** doit à son limon quaternaire une extraordinaire fertilité. À la culture des céréales et des betteraves sucrières succèdent, sur les molles ondulations de la partie orientale, les herbages plantés d'arbres fruitiers. Au printemps, les villages sont cernés par les fleurs des vergers. Ceux de Kuttekoven sont serrés autour de l'église paroissiale qui a gardé sa belle tour romane.

The peneplain of the **Hesbaye**, athwart a linguistic frontier, owes its great fertility to the alluvial deposits of the Quaternary era. In the gently rolling countryside of the eastern portion pastures planted with fruit trees replace cereals and sugar beets. In springtime villages such as **Kuttekoven**, grouped around its parish church with a pretty Romanesque tower, are surrounded by a sea of blossom.

Die Fastebene von **Hespengau** — hier treffen niederländische und französische Sprache aufeinander — verdankt ihre außerordentliche Fruchtbarkeit den aus der Quatärzeit stammenden Schlammformationen. Den Getreide- und Zuckerrübenkulturen folgen auf den sanften Hügeln des östlichen Gebiets mit Obstbäumen bestandene Wiesen. Im Frühjahr sind die Dörfer von blühenden Obstgärten umgeben. Die von Kuttekoven drängen sich um die Dorfkirche, deren schöner romanischer Turm bis heute erhalten blieb.

◁ Het huis „Het Sweert" werd reeds vernoemd in de stadsarchieven van **Hasselt**. Het is een schoolvoorbeeld van de Romaanse stijl in het Maasbekken. Zoals het jaartal op de gevel aanduidt, kreeg het gebouw in 1659 zijn huidige uitzicht met vakwerk in Sint-Andreaskruis in de bovenverdieping. Op de hoek van de tweede verdieping zwaait een gemaskerde en gehandschoende man met een zwaard. Tot in 1713 was het huis een herberg. Daarna kreeg het zijn huidige bestemming : een apotheek.

Déjà citée dans un document d'archives de **Hasselt**, la maison *Het Sweert* (l'Epée) constitue un témoignage exemplaire du style mosan. Comme l'indique un millésime, c'est en 1659 que l'édifice prit son aspect actuel avec ses colombages et croix de Saint-André dans sa partie supérieure. À l'angle du deuxième étage, une main gantée brandit une épée derrière une tête masquée. La maison était une auberge jusqu'en 1713, date à partir de laquelle elle devint une pharmacie. Elle l'est toujours.

The building called *Het Sweert* (the Sword), a prime example of the Mosan style, is mentioned in the archives of **Hasselt**. As may be seen by the date the building received its present aspect with half-timbered cross stays on the upper storey in 1659. On the corner of the second floor a gloved hand brandishes a sword behind a masked head. The building was an inn until 1713 when it became a pharmacy as it is today.

Das bereits in einem Archivdokument von **Hasselt** erwähnte Haus mit Namen *Het Sweert* (das Schwert) stellt ein ausgezeichnetes Zeugnis maasländischen Stils dar. Wie eine Jahreszahl angibt, erhielt das Gebäude seine derzeitige Gestalt mit Andreas-Kreuz-Säulen im oberen Teil im Jahre 1659. An der Ecke der zweiten Etage hält eine mit einem Handschuh versehene Hand ein Schwert hinter einem maskierten Kopf. Bis 1713 war das Haus eine Herberge. Seitdem wird es als Apotheke genutzt.

△ De in zekere mate van het cultuurgebeuren afgesneden Kempen bleven «trouw aan een nederig verleden». Daar bestaan nog uitgestrekte natuurreservaten. In het openluchtmuseum van **Bokrijk** heeft men oude hoeven, schuren, kapellen en molens uit de Vlaamse gouwen samengebracht en zo van vernieling gespaard.

Son éloignement des grandes voies historiques de civilisation laissa longtemps la Campine «fidèle à un humble passé». Il y subsiste de vastes réserves naturelles. Dans le musée de plein air du domaine de **Bokrijk** on a remonté et sauvé de la destruction des fermes, des granges, des chapelles et des moulins provenant de provinces flamandes.

As it lay far removed from the mainstream of civilisation, the Kempen area was for a long time «faithful to its humble past». Here there are large nature reserves. Farms, barns, chapels and mills from all parts of Flanders have been saved from destruction and reconstructed in the open air museum of the **Bokrijk** estate.

Seine Entfernung von den großen historischen Straßen der Zivilisation ließ das Kempenland lange «einer demütigen Vergangenheit treu» bleiben. Dort bestehen noch ausgedehnte Naturschutzgebiete. Im Freiluftmuseum der Domäne **Bokrijk** wurden Bauernhäuser, Scheunen, Kapellen und Mühlen, die aus flämischen Provinzen stammen, wieder aufgebaut und vor der Zerstörung gerettet.

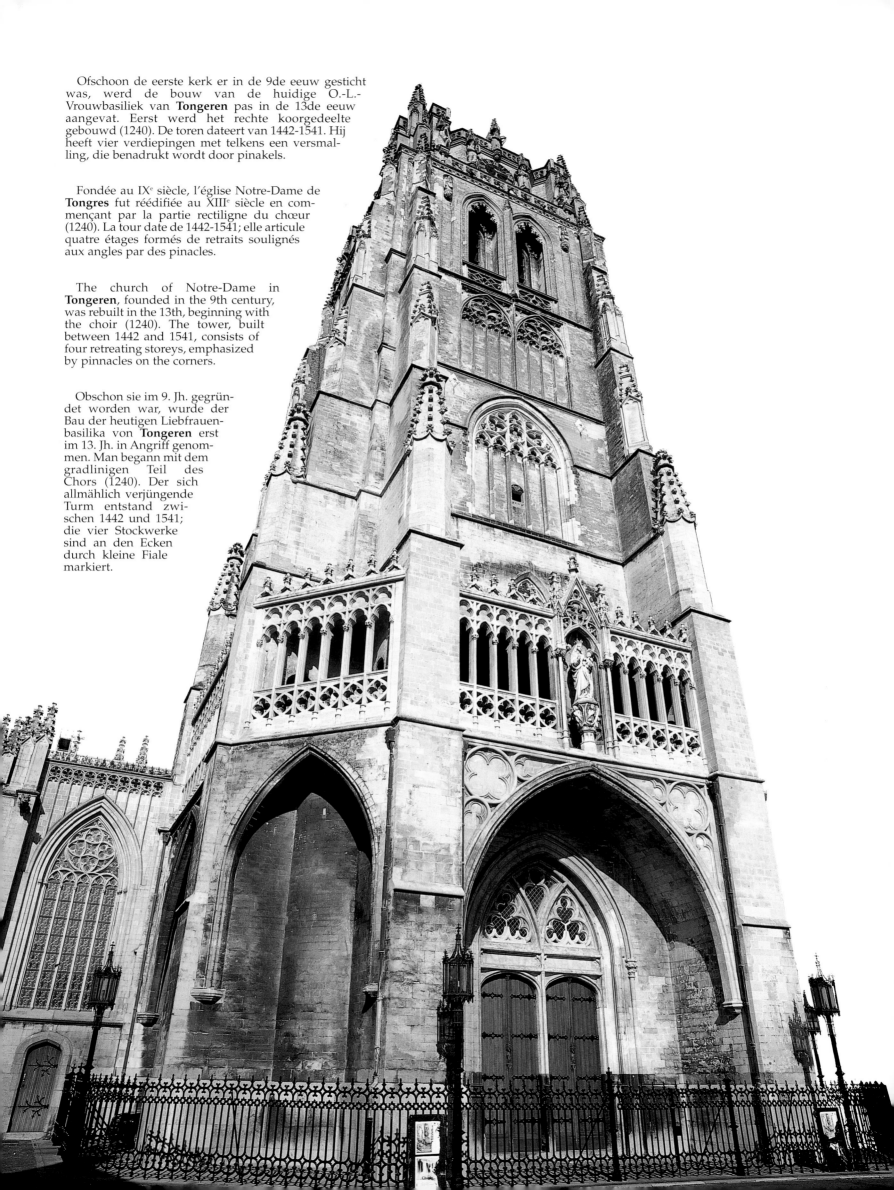

Ofschoon de eerste kerk er in de 9de eeuw gesticht was, werd de bouw van de huidige O.-L.-Vrouwbasiliek van **Tongeren** pas in de 13de eeuw aangevat. Eerst werd het rechte koorgedeelte gebouwd (1240). De toren dateert van 1442-1541. Hij heeft vier verdiepingen met telkens een versmalling, die benadrukt wordt door pinakels.

Fondée au IXe siècle, l'église Notre-Dame de **Tongres** fut réédifiée au XIIIe siècle en commençant par la partie rectiligne du chœur (1240). La tour date de 1442-1541; elle articule quatre étages formés de retraits soulignés aux angles par des pinacles.

The church of Notre-Dame in **Tongeren**, founded in the 9th century, was rebuilt in the 13th, beginning with the choir (1240). The tower, built between 1442 and 1541, consists of four retreating storeys, emphasized by pinnacles on the corners.

Obschon sie im 9. Jh. gegründet worden war, wurde der Bau der heutigen Liebfrauenbasilika von **Tongeren** erst im 13. Jh. in Angriff genommen. Man begann mit dem gradlinigen Teil des Chors (1240). Der sich allmählich verjüngende Turm entstand zwischen 1442 und 1541; die vier Stockwerke sind an den Ecken durch kleine Fiale markiert.

Het 17de-eeuwse stadhuis van het stadje **Peer** toont een evenwichtig samenspel tussen gotiek en barok. Op het eind van de 18de eeuw kreeg het stadhuis bekendheid ten gevolge van de processen die er zich voltrokken tegen de *Bokkenrijders*, roversbendes die terreur zaaiden in Limburg. De mensen geloofden dat ze 's nachts, gezeten op bokken, door de lucht vlogen. Een zekere Holleke van Geleen, afkomstig uit Bree, werd in dit gebouw gemarteld. Na zijn terdoodveroordeling werd hij in Pelt terechtgesteld.

Dans la petite cité de **Peer**, l'hôtel de ville du XVIIe siècle mêle habilement les styles gothiques et baroques. À la fin du XVIIIe siècle, il connut une sinistre célébrité à la suite des procès qui s'y déroulèrent contre les *Bokkenrijders*, bandes de brigands qui semaient la terreur dans le Limbourg. Les gens croyaient que, la nuit, ils volaient dans les airs, chevauchant des boucs *(bokken)*. Un certain Holleke van Geleen originaire de Bree fut torturé dans l'édifice. Condamné à mort, il fut exécuté à Pelt.

In the small town of **Peer** the 17th century town hall is a pleasant mixture of Gothic and baroque styles. At the end of the 18th century it gained notoriety as the scene of the prosecution of the *Bokkenrijders*, bands of brigands that terrorised the Limbourg. People believed that at night they flew through the air mounted on billy-goats or *bokken*. One Holleke van Geelen from Bree was tortured in this building. He received the death penalty and was executed in Pelt.

Das Rathaus der kleinen Stadt **Peer** verbindet auf geschickte Weise gotische und barocke Elemente. Zum Ende des 18. Jahrhunderts wurde es infolge der Prozesse, die dort gegen die *Bokkenrijders*, eine Räuberbande, die Limburg in Angst und Schrecken versetzte, geführt wurden, berühmt berüchtigt. Die Menschen glaubten, dass die Räuber nachts auf Ziegenböcken *(bokken)* durch die Luft ritten. Ein gewisser aus Bree stammender Holleke van Geleen wurde in dem Gebäude gefoltert. Nach seiner Verurteilung zum Tode wurde er in Pelt hingerichtet.

De aan de Maas gelegen stad **Maaseik** heeft haar bekendheid hoofdzakelijk te danken aan de gebroeders Van Eyck, die er geboren zouden zijn. Rond het marktplein met zijn dubbele rij lindebomen, net zoals in de naburige straten van het vroeger tot het prinsbisdom Luik behorende stadje, zijn talrijke zeer fraaie Maaslandse gevels bewaard gebleven.

La réputation de **Maaseik**, sur les rives de la Meuse, est liée à celle des frères van Eyck qui y seraient nés. De surcroît, sur la grand-place plantée de tilleuls, la petite ville principautaire possède de splendides façades de style mosan. D'autres, non moins remarquables, sont dispersées le long des rues.

Maaseik, on the banks of the Meuse, is known principally as the birth place of the van Eyck brothers. On the town square, shaded by lime trees, are splendid Mosan façades and others, just as remarkable, may be found along the neighbouring streets.

Maaseik, an den Ufern der Maas, ist vor allem als vermutlicher Geburtsort der Brüder Van Eyck bekannt. Prächtige Häusergiebel in maasländischem Stil umgeben den Marktplatz mit der schönen Lindenallee und stehen entlang der Straßen.

En l'église romane de **Saint-Séverin** (XIIe siècle) se mêlent sans jamais se contredire les influences rhénanes et bourguignonnes. Les trois absidioles qui prolongent la travée du chœur et les bas-côtés apportent un élément de charme au robuste édifice clunisien.

De Romaanse kerk van **Saint-Séverin** (12de eeuw) is een voorbeeld van het harmonieus samengaan van Rijnlandse en Bourgondische invloeden. De drie kleine absissen geven het kloeke bouwwerk in de stijl van Cluny een vriendelijker aanzicht.

The Romanesque church of **Saint-Séverin** (12th century) is a happy combination of Rhenish and Burgundian influences. The three small apses which prolong the bay of the choir and the aisles, add grace to the robust Cluniac edifice.

In der romanischen Kirche in **Saint-Séverin** (12. Jh.) mischen sich widerspruchslos die rheinischen und burgundischen Einflüsse. Die drei Chornischen, die das Chorjoch und die Seitenschiffe verlängern, geben dem kräftigen clunizianischen Bau einen gewinnenden Reiz.

Jean-Gaspard de Marchin (1652-1673) s'était illustré sur les champs de bataille aux côtés du prince de Condé. Son courage était légendaire mais, à la cour de France, on riait de sa vanité. Comme pour répondre aux moqueries, le comte de Marchin multiplia les armoiries en son **château de Modave**. Dans le grand vestibule ou salle des gardes, il fit décorer le plafond de son arbre généalogique et de trente-deux quartiers de noblesse, et, sur le manteau de la cheminée, il fit sculpter un extrait du *Miroir des Nobles du Hainaut*.

Jean-Gaspard de Marchin (1652-1673) distinguished himself on the battlefield at the side of the Prince of Condé. His courage was legendary but the French court was amused by his vainglory. As a response to the mockery he had incurred Count Marchin displayed his armorial bearings ostentatiously in his home, **Modave castle**. He had the ceiling of the great vestibule or guard room decorated with his family tree and thirty-two quarterings of nobility. An excerpt from The Mirror of the Nobles of Hainaut was carved on the chimneypiece.

Jean-Gaspard de Marchin (1652-1673) had zich op het slagveld onderscheiden aan de zijde van de prins van Condé. Zijn moed was legendarisch, maar aan het Franse hof lachte men om zijn ijdelheid. Misschien was het om die spotternijen van antwoord te dienen dat de graaf van Marchin het aantal wapenschilden in zijn **kasteel te Modave** nog verder uitbreidde. In de grote inkomhal of wachtzaal, liet hij het plafond versieren met zijn stamboom en met 32 kwartieren. Op de schoorsteenmantel liet hij een uittreksel beeldhouwen van de *Spiegel der Henegouwse adel*.

Jean-Gaspard von Marchin (1652-1673) gelangte an der Seite des Prinzen von Condé auf den Schlachtfeldern zu Ruhm. Sein Mut war legendär, doch am französischen Hof mokierte man sich über seine Eitelkeit. Wie zur Bestätigung dieses Spotts ließ er in seinem **Schloss von Modave** zusätzliche Wappen anfertigen. In der großen Vorhalle oder im Wachsaal ließ er die Decke mit seinem Stammbaum und zweiunddreißig Adelsnachweisen dekorieren, und auf dem Kamin ließ er einen Auszug aus *Miroir des Nobles du Hainaut* hauen.

◁

L'hôtel que Nicolas Willems construisit en Féronstrée, au XVIIIᵉ siècle, reçut le nom du comte d'Ansembourg lorsque la petite-fille du banquier liégeois fit alliance avec cette famille. C'est l'actuel **musée d'art décoratif de Liège**. La richesse de l'ornementation intérieure, notamment celle des plafonds peints, entoure désormais les collections du XVIIIᵉ siècle, qui intègrent avec finesse le style français pour en faire un style Régence liégeois d'une évidente originalité.

Dit in de 18de eeuw door N. Willems in Féronstrée gebouwde herenhuis erfde de naam van de graven van Ansembourg, toen de kleindochter van de Luikse bankier in die familie inhuwde. Het is thans het **Decoratie-museum van Luik**. Pracht en praal van de binnenverzorging, o.a. van de beschilderde plafonds, omkaderen als het ware de verza-melingen uit de 18de eeuw, waarvan de bevalligheid die van de Franse voorbeelden evenaart en een typisch Luiks tintje aan de régencestijl verleent.

The mansion built at Féronstrée in the 18th century by Nicholas Willems, a Liège banker, received the name of the Count of Ansem-bourg when his granddaughter married into that family. The richness of the interior orna-mentation, particularly the painted ceilings, is an adaptation of French style in a highly original Liège Regency manner and serves as a fitting setting for the 18th century collec-tions of the **Museum of Decorative Arts of Liège**.

Das herrschaftliche Haus, das N. Willems im 18. Jh. in Féronstrée baute, erhielt den Namen des Grafen d'Ansembourg, als die Enkelin des Lütticher Bankiers in dessen Familie einheiratete. Heute ist es das **Museum für Dekorationskunst von Lüttich**. Die prachtvolle Innenausstattung mit bemalten Zimmerdecken lässt die angehäuften Kunstgegenstände aus dem 18. Jh. vortrefflich zur Geltung kommen. Die Eleganz des französischen Régencestils erhält hier eine für die Lütticher Gegend ty-pische Prägung.

▷

Dressée en 1697 sur la **place du Marché à Liège** par Jean Del Cour, la fontaine du **Perron**, symbole des libertés communales, est dominée par trois Grâces portant la pomme de pin celtique surmontée d'une croix.

Sinds 1697 prijkt op het **Marktplein te Luik** de **Perron** fontein, symbool der gemeentelijke vrijheden, opgericht door Jean Del Cour. De groep der drie Gratiën draagt een Keltische pijnappel met een kruis erop.

The **Perron** fountain, built in the **Market square of Liège** in 1697 by Jean Del Cour, symbolises the municipal liberties. At the summit, three Graces support a Celtic pine-cone topped with a crucifix.

Den **Perron-Brunnen**, den Jean Del Cour 1697 auf dem **Lütticher Marktplatz** als Sinnbild der städtischen Freiheit errichtete, überragen drei Grazien, die den keltischen Pinienzapfen mit einem Kreuz darauf tra-gen.

◁

Commencée au XVᵉ siècle, l'**église Saint-Jacques** à **Liège** fut achevée durant la première moitié du siècle suivant. Ses nefs, en particulier leurs voûtes, ont bénéficié d'une décoration très riche. Surbaissées, celles-ci sont ornées soit d'un réseau de moulures en treillis, soit de motifs en forme d'étoile, de fleur ou de feuillage.

De oprichting van de **St-Jacobuskerk** in **Luik** begon in de 15de eeuw, maar de kerk werd pas in de eerste helft van de 16de voltooid. De beuken, vooral de beschilderde gewelven hebben een zeer weelderig effect. Deze ingebogen gewelven zijn ofwel met lijstwerk versierd ofwel met ster-, bloem- of bladvormige motieven overzaaid.

Begun in **Liège** in the 15th century and completed during the first half of the 16th, **St. James** church boasts richly decorated naves and vaults. The flattened vaults are ornamented either with a network of moulded trelliswork or with star, flower or leaf motifs.

Der Bau der **St.-Jakobskirche** in **Lüttich** wurde im 15. Jh. in Angriff genommen, doch das Gotteshaus wurde erst in der ersten Hälfte des 16. Jh. vollendet. Der Innenraum, vor allem die Gewölbe, wurden prachtvoll ausgeschmückt. Die recht flach konstruierten Gewölbe sind zum Teil in ein Raster von plastisch gestalteten Rippen eingespannt, zum Teil mit stern-, blumen- oder blattförmigen Motiven bemalt.

▷

Avec ses rues abruptes et ses jardins en terrasses, Liège s'étage sur les coteaux des hauteurs qui la ceignent. Les quatre cents degrés de l'impressionnante **Montagne de Bueren** montent à la citadelle, posée sur l'une des trois collines qui gardent la Cité Ardente.

De steile straten van Luik en de terrastuinen lopen trapsgewijs op tegen de hellingen van de heuvels die de stad omringen. De vierhonderd treden van de indrukwekkende **Montagne de Bueren** leiden naar de vesting van de stad, gelegen op één van de drie voornaamste heuvels van Luik.

The steep streets and terraced gardens of Liège mount the slope of the surrounding hills. The 400 steps of the impressive **"Bueren mountain"** rise to the Citadel, perched on one of the three hills which guard the "cité ardente".

Die steilen Straßen und die Terrassengärten der Stadt steigen stufenweise die Abhänge der Hügel hinauf, die Lüttich umschließen. Die imposanten vierhundert Stufen der **Montagne de Bueren** führen zur Festung der Stadt, die sich auf einer der drei Anhöhen erstreckt, auf denen Lüttich gebaut wurde.

◁
(Page de gauche)
À **Limbourg**, petite ville quiète perchée sur les hauteurs, on imagine malaisément qu'on foule le sol d'une ancienne capitale de duché. Les sobres maisons bourgeoises qui entourent la place n'évoquent en rien la redoutable forteresse d'antan, assiégée par les Normands, les Espagnols et les Français qui la détruisirent en 1703.

(Linkerbladzijde)
Als men in het rustige, hooggelegen stadje **Limbourg** rondkuiert, valt het moeilijk zich voor te stellen dat men voet heeft gezet op de bodem van de hoofdstad van een oud hertogdom. De onopvallende herenhuizen rond het plein doen hoegenaamd niet denken aan de schrikwekkende burcht, die achtereenvolgens door de Noormannen, de Spanjaarden en de Fransen werd bestormd, alvorens ze in 1703 door Franse troepen werd vernield.

(Left page)
In **Limbourg**, a quiet little town perched on a hill, it is hard to imagine that you are treading the soil of the capital of a former Duchy. The austere middle-class houses around the square give no inkling of the formidable fortress of long ago, besieged by the Normans, the Spanish and the French, who destroyed it in 1703.

(Linke Seite)
Es fällt einem schwer, im stillen, auf Anhöhen gelagerten Städtchen **Limbourg** das Gefühl zu haben, dass man den Boden der alten Hauptstadt eines Herzogtums betreten hat. Die unauffälligen Bürgerhäuser, die den Platz umgeben, dürften kaum die Erinnerung an die berüchtigte Festung von früher wachrufen, die von den Normannen, den Spaniern und den Franzosen belagert wurde, bis letztere sie 1703 zerstörten.

Les deux tours aux toitures baroques de l'église Saint-Nicolas dominent la ville d'**Eupen** dont le passé et le folklore sont évoqués dans les salles du Musée communal *(en bas)*. Cette belle demeure patricienne fut construite en 1697, quelque trente ans avant l'église.

De stad **Eupen** wordt gedomineerd door de twee torens met barokke daken van de Sint-Niklaaskerk. Het verleden en de folkore van de stad worden in beeld gebracht in het stadsmuseum *(hieronder)*. Deze mooie patriciërswoning werd gebouwd in 1697, zo'n 30 jaar voor de kerk.

The two baroque-roofed towers of Saint Nicholas' church in **Eupen** dominate the town whose past and folklore are evoked in the Municipal Museum *(below)*. This fine patrician residence was built in 1697, some thirty years before the church.

Die beiden mit Barockdächern geschmückten Türme der Sankt-Nikolaus-Kirche beherrschen die Stadt **Eupen**, deren Vergangenheit und Volkskunde in den Räumen des Stadtmuseums *(unten)* zu entdecken sind. Dieses schöne Patrizierhaus wurde 1697, rund dreißig Jahre vor der Kirche errichtet.

(Double page suivante)
Aux **Fonds-de-Quareux**, l'Amblève a creusé une gorge étroite à travers le massif hercynien couvert de forêts. Arrachés de la montagne par l'action érosive des eaux, les blocs de quartzite sont éparpillés dans le lit de la rivière écumante.

(Volgende dubbele bladzijde)
In de **Fonds-de-Quareux** heeft de Amblève een diepe bergengte uitgegraven in het beboste ertsgebergte. Enorme blokken kwartssteen, door de erosieve werking van het water uit de bergen losgemaakt, liggen verspreid in de bedding van de schuimende rivier.

(Next two pages)
The river Amblève has carved out a narrow gorge through the wooded rocky massif. The **Fonds-de-Quareux**, great blocks of quartz, have been torn from the mountain by the erosive action of the river and lie amid the foaming water.

(Nächste Doppelseite)
Im **Fonds-de-Quareux** grub die Amel eine enge Schlucht durch das mit Wäldern bedeckte herzynische Gebirge. Durch die fressende Wirkung der Gewässer vom Berg abgerissen, sind die Quarzablagerungen im schäumenden Flussbett verstreut.

Les grandes fermes étaient rares en Ardenne. Pour lutter contre la rudesse du climat, on y construisait les maisons à un étage en maçonnant des murs de moellons d'au moins cinquante centimètres comme à **Xhoffraix** *(page de gauche, en haut)*, soit, dans la vallée de l'Amblève, en utilisant le bois, la brique, le torchis et le colombage comme à **Ster** prés de Stavelot *(page de gauche, en bas)*.
(Ci-dessus)

Stavelot, c'est l'ancienne abbaye bénédictine, siège de la principauté ecclésiastique, la châsse de saint Remacle, la fontaine du Perron, le musée Guillaume Apollinaire mais c'est aussi de larges perspectives sur les campagnes et les forêts qui entourent l'amphithéâtre que la ville forme sur la rive droite de l'Amblève. En automne, feuillus et mélèzes offrent le spectacle d'immenses bouquets fauves parmi le vert persistant des autres conifères.

Grote boerderijen waren zeldzaam in de Ardennen. Om zich te wapenen tegen het strenge klimaat bouwde men er huizen met slechts één verdieping en met breukstenen van minstens 50 cm dik, zoals in **Xhoffraix** *(linkerbladzijde, bovenaan)*. Ofwel gebruikte men, zoals in de vallei van de Amblève, hout, baksteen, leem en vakwerk. Een voorbeeld hiervan vindt men in **Ster**, nabij Stavelot *(linkerbladzijde, onderaan)*.
(Hierboven)

Stavelot wordt geassocieerd met de vroegere benedictijnerabdij, de zetel van het kerkelijk prinsdom, het reliekschrijn van Sint Remaclus, de fontein van het perron, het museum Guillaume Apollinaire, maar het staat eveneens synoniem voor platteland en wouden die de amfitheatervormige stad op de rechteroever van de Amblève omringen. In de herfst vormen de loofbomen en lorken een immens roest boeket tussen de altijdgroene naaldbomen.

Large farmhouses were rare in the Ardennes. One storey houses with grouted walls in undressed stone at least fifty centimeters thick were built to combat the rigorous climate as can be seen at **Xhoffraix** *(upper page left)* or in a mixture of wood, brick, cob and half-timbering as at **Ster** in the Amblève valley near Stavelot *(lower page left)*.
(Above)

Stavelot is the site of the old Benedictine abbey, the reliquary of Saint Remacle, the Perron fountain, the Guillaume Apollinaire Museum and once the seat of an ecclesiastical principality. It commands wide views of the fields and forests surrounding the amphitheatre of the town on the right bank of the Amblève. In autumn the broad-leafed trees and larches look like gigantic tawny bouquets among the evergreens.

Große Bauernhöfe gab es in den Ardennen nur wenige. Zum Schutz gegen die Härte des Klimas baute man dort einstöckige Häuser, deren Wände mit Bruchsteinen von mindestens fünfzig Zentimetern versehen wurden, wie etwa in **Xhoffraix** *(linke Seite, oben)*, oder aber im Amblève-Tal mit Holz, Backsteinen, Strohlehm und Fachwerk wie etwa in **Ster** in der Nähe von Stavelot *(linke Seite, unten)*.
(Oben)

Stavelot beherbergt eine ehemalige Benediktinerabtei, den Sitz des geistlichen Fürstentums, den Schrein des Heiligen Remacle, den Freitreppen-Brunnen sowie das Guillaume Apollinaire-Museum. Zudem bietet es eine weite Aussicht über die Felder und Wälder, die das Amphitheater, das die Stadt am rechten Amblève-Ufer bildet, umgeben. Im Herbst bieten die Laubbäume und Lärchen den Anblick riesiger fahlroter Blumensträuße unter dem bleibenden Grün der übrigen Koniferen.

△▷
À l'emplacement d'un fond marin de l'époque cambrienne, soulevé puis érodé et abrasé au cours de dizaines de millions d'années, les **Hautes Fagnes** sont le toit de la Belgique. Elles atteignent près de sept cents mètres à Botrange. Exceptionnelles, leur faune et leur flore sont de caractère boréal et montagnard.
(Page de droite)
L'église d'Ouren.

De **Hoge Venen** — ten tijde van het Cambrium nog zeebodem — zijn in de loop der millennia ontstaan ten gevolge van prehistorische bodemopstuwingen, erosie en abrasie. Thans worden ze terecht het dak van België genoemd. Bij Botrange liggen ze zowat 700 m boven de zeespiegel. De uitzonderlijke fauna en flora doen denken aan het hoge noorden en aan bergstreken.
(Rechterbladzijde)
De kerk van Ouren.

Rising to nearly 700 meters at Botrange, the **Hautes Fagnes** are called "the roof of Belgium", but during the Cambrian period they were a sea bottom which, over hundreds of thousands of years, rose from the depths, was abraded and eroded. The flora and fauna have unusual boreal and alpine characteristics.
(Right page)
The church at Ouren.

Im Kambrium war die Gegend des **Hohen Venns** noch Meeresgrund. Im Laufe der Jahrtausende der Vorgeschichte entstand hier durch Erdbewegungen, -abtragungen und -erosion das „Dach Belgiens", das sich bei Botrange nahezu 700 m über dem Meeresspiegel erhebt. Die Tier- und Pflanzenwelt weisen Übereinstimmungen mit denen nordischer und gebirgiger Gegenden auf.
(Rechte Seite)
Die Kirche von Ouren.

(Double page suivante)
Du château de **Reuland**, berceau d'une des plus anciennes familles féodales de l'Eifel, il demeure une tour qui surplombe les toits d'ardoises du village tassé autour de son église au clocher bulbeux (1712).

(Volgende dubbele bladzijde)
Van het kasteel van **Reuland**, bakermat van één van de oudste feodale families uit de Eifel, bestaat nog een toren die uitziet over de leistenen daken van de dorpshuizen, geschaard rond de kerk met bolvormige klokkentoren (1712).

(Next two pages)
Of the castle in **Reuland**, which was the seat of one of the oldest feudal families in the Eifel region, all that is left is a tower which dominates the slate roofs of the village and the church with its bulbous tower (1712).

(Nächste Doppelseite)
Von der Burg in **Reuland**, der Wiege eines der ältesten Feudalgeschlechter der Eifel, steht noch ein Turm, der die Schieferdächer des um seine Kirche mit dem Zwiebelturm (1712) gescharten Dorfes überragt.

Il est peu de paysages aussi pathétiques et aussi vrais que la crête du **Hérou**, à quelques lieues du confluent des deux Ourthes. Les collines paraissent se bousculer autour des bras multiples de la rivière.

Geen pathetischer en tegelijk geen onvervalster landschap dan de bergkam van **Hérou**, niet ver van de samenloop der beide Ourthes. De heuvelruggen schijnen zich rond de talrijke armen der rivier te verdringen.

There is in Belgium no more moving landscape than the **Hérou** ridge, a few miles from the junction of the two Ourthes rivers. Here the hills seem to jostle for space among the multiple arms of the river.

Es gibt wenig so ergreifende und gleichzeitig so urtümliche Landschaften wie den **Hérou**-Kamm, einige Meilen vom Zusammenfluss der beiden Ourthen entfernt. Die Hügel scheinen sich buchstäblich um die zahlreichen Arme des Flusses zu drängen.

(Pages 80 à 82)
Nichée dans une courbe de l'Ourthe face à de splendides rochers aux plissements parallèles, la petite ville de **Durbuy** peut se vanter d'être au cœur d'une région habitée depuis les temps les plus reculés.

(Blz. 80 tot 82)
Diep weggedoken in een bocht van de Ourthe, uitkijkend op schitterende rotsformaties, ligt het stadje **Durbuy** in het hart van een streek die erop kan bogen sinds mensenheugenis bewoond te zijn.

(Pages 80 to 82)
Nestled in a curve of the river Ourthe, facing an impressive rock formation with parallel folding, the small town of **Durbuy** prides itself on being the centre of a region that has been inhabited since the earliest times.

(Seiten 80 bis 82)
In einer Kurve der Ourthe gegenüber prächtigen Felsen mit gebogenen Falten eingenistet, kann sich das Städtchen **Durbuy** rühmen, im Herzen einer seit den ältesten Zeiten bewohnten Gegend zu liegen.

(Page 87)
Le promontoire rocheux que contourne l'Ourthe a été occupé par les Celtes, les Romains et les Francs avant que Henri, fils cadet du comte de Namur, n'y plante une forteresse au début du XIIᵉ siècle. Les murailles du château de **La Roche-en-Ardenne** épousaient les déclivités du rocher pour former des plates-formes. Les troupes de Louis XIV dévastèrent l'ensemble, ne laissant subsister que les tours d'angle.

(Blz. 87)
Het rotsachtig voorgebergte, waar de Ourthe omheen stroomt, werd bewoond door Kelten, Romeinen en Franken tot Henri, de jongste zoon van de graaf van Namen, er in het begin van de 12de eeuw een vesting op neerplantte. De vestingmuren van het kasteel van **La Roche-en-Ardenne** volgen de glooiingen van de rotsen om plateaus te vormen. De troepen van Lodewijk XIV vernielden het geheel en lieten enkel de hoektorens overeind staan.

(Page 87)
The Ourthe flows around a rocky promontory occupied successively by the Celts, Romans and Franks. In the 12th century Henri, younger son of the Count of Namur, built a fortress on it. The high walls of the castle of **La Roche-en-Ardenne** followed the declivity of the rock, creating enclosed platforms. The troops of Louis XIV destroyed the castle, leaving only the corner towers.

(Seite 87)
Das felsige Vorgebirge, durch das sich die Ourthe schlängelt, stand unter keltischer, römischer und fränkischer Besatzung, ehe Heinrich, der jüngste Sohn des Grafen von Namur, dort Anfang des 12. Jh. eine Festung errichten ließ. Die Mauern der Festung **La Roche-en-Ardenne** sind in die steilen Felswände integriert und bilden Plateaus. Die Truppen unter Ludwig XIV. verwüsteten die Anlage, wobei nur die Ecktürme stehenblieben.

Non loin de Paliseul, le village ardennais de **Dochamps** tasse autour de l'église ses maisons aux toits d'ardoises. L'architecture rurale en est stricte, rugueuse, sans prétention comme les habitants.

Niet ver van Paliseul ligt het Ardense dorp **Dochamps**. De landelijke bouwstijl van de huizen, die zich met hun leien daken als het ware verdringen rond de kerk, weerspiegelt de ietwat stroeve, strenge eenvoud van de bewoners.

The rural architecture of the Ardennes village of **Dochamps** with its slate roofed houses clustered around the church is as honest, study and unpretentious as its inhabitants.

Das Ardenner Dorf **Dochamps** liegt nicht weit von Paliseul entfernt. Die Häuser mit ihren Schieferdächern sind dicht an dicht um die Kirche herum gebaut. Der schlichte, fast herbe, alles Großtuerische vermeidende Baustil spiegelt den Charakter der Bewohner wider.

Jouxtant le Fourneau Saint-Michel, ancien complexe métallurgique, un **musée de la Vie rurale** a été créé le long de la Masblette. Il permet de reconstruire avec les matériaux d'origine, soigneusement démontés, maintes maisons ardennaises qui étaient condamnées à la destruction.

Dicht bij Fourneau Saint-Michel, een buiten bedrijf gesteld metaalverwerkend complex, werd langs de oevers van de Masblette een **museum van het plattelandsleven** in het leven geroepen. Talrijke Ardense huizen, die bestemd waren voor de sloophamer, werden zorgvuldig afgebroken en daar opnieuw met de oorspronkelijke materialen opgebouwd.

A **Museum of Rural Life** has been established next to the Fourneau Saint-Michel, an ancient metal works on the banks of the Masblette. Many old houses from the Ardennes, doomed to destruction, have been carefully dismantled and reconstructed using the original material.

In unmittelbarer Nähe des stillgelegten Hüttenbetriebs Fourneau Saint-Michel wurde am Ufer der Masblette entlang ein **Museum des bäuerlichen Lebens** eingerichtet. Zahlreiche, sorgfältig Stein um Stein abgetragene Häuser aus den Ardennen, die sonst niedergerissen worden wären, sind hier mit den ursprünglichen Baumaterialien zu neuem Leben wiedererstanden.

◁

La basilique de **Saint-Hubert** (1526-1564) occupe l'emplacement d'un sanctuaire du XIIe siècle qui, sauf la crypte, brûla dans l'incendie de 1524. La longue nef gothique de l'église est séparée de ses bas-côtés par des piliers nervurés, dépourvus de chapiteaux. Le remplage du triforium se prolonge jusque dans les écoinçons des arcatures. Le chœur, très profond, est surélevé et surmonte une crypte où était vénérée la châsse de saint Hubert aujourd'hui disparue.

De basiliek van **Saint-Hubert** (1526-1564) staat precies op de plaats van een vroeger heiligdom uit de 12de eeuw dat — behalve de crypte — onderging in de brand van 1524. De lange hoofdbeuk van de kerk is van de zijbeuken gescheiden door geribde pilaren zonder kapitelen. De opvulling van het triforium reikt tot aan de blindboogjes die als hoekversiering dienen. Het lange koor is verhoogd en verheft zich boven een crypte waar het thans zoek geraakte reliekschrijn van de heilige Hubertus werd vereerd.

The basilica of **Saint-Hubert**, dating from 1526-1564, was built on the site of a 12th century sanctuary which, except for the crypt, was burnt out completely in the fire of 1524. The long Gothic nave of the church is separated from its aisles by ribbed pillars, without capitals. The triforium backing extends into the spandrels of the arcades. The deep chancel is raised over a crypt where the reliquary of Saint Hubert used to be worshipped before it disappeared.

Die Basilika von **Saint-Hubert** wurde 1526-1564 erbaut und steht an der Stelle einer Kirche aus dem 12. Jh., die mit Ausnahme der Krypta 1524 niederbrannte. Das lange gotische Mittelschiff der Kirche ist durch Bündelpfeiler ohne Kapitelle von den Seitenschiffen getrennt. Die Mauerfüllung des Triforiums dringt bis in die Eckverblendung mittels Bogenwerk vor. Der erhöhte, sehr lange Chor erhebt sich über einer Krypta, in der der inzwischen abhanden gekommene Reliquienschrein des heiligen Hubertus verehrt wurde.

△

Perché sur un promontoire rocheux que cerne la Semois, le château fort de **Bouillon** remonte sans doute à la seconde moitié du IXe siècle mais il fut partiellement rebâti au XVIe siècle, après le siège par le comte de Nassau en 1521. Le donjon est contemporain de Godefroid, le héros de la première Croisade.

Op een overhellende rots boven de Semois troont het slot van **Bouillon**, sinds de tweede helft van de 9de eeuw. Het werd echter gedeeltelijk herbouwd in de 16de eeuw na het beleg van de Graaf van Nassau in 1521. De toren dateert uit de tijd van Godfried van Bouillon, de held van de eerste Kruistocht.

Perched a rocky promontory washed by the waters of the Semois, the stronghold of **Bouillon** is believed to date from the second half of the 9th century but was partly rebuilt in the 16th century after being besieged by the Count of Nassau, in 1521. The keep dates back to Godfrey, the hero of the first Crusade.

Auf einem von der Semois umschlossenen Vorgebirge erhebt sich die Burg **Bouillon**, die wahrscheinlich aus der zweiten Hälfte des 9. Jh. stammt, aber im 16. Jh. nach der Belagerung durch den Grafen von Nassau im Jahre 1521 teilweise neu gebaut wurde. Der Wartturm stammt aus der Zeit Gottfrieds, des Helden des ersten Kreuzzuges.

De tous les sites d'entre-Semois-et-Vierre, celui de **Chassepierre** a le plus inspiré les peintres de la Gaume. Caché dans une gorge encaissée, le village doit être vu de haut. Les toits d'ardoise font alors une harmonieuse escorte à l'église romane Saint-Martin qui a reçu en 1702 un clocher bulbeux baroque.

Van alle tussen de Semois en de Vierre gelegen landschappen heeft **Chassepierre** de schilders van de Gaume het meest geïnspireerd. Als men het in een bergengte verscholen dorp vanuit de hoogte bekijkt, bevalt het beter. De leien daken harmoniëren dan met de Romaanse Sint-Maartenskerk, die in 1702 van een barokke, bolvormige klokkentoren werd voorzien.

Of all the sites between the Semois and the Vierre, the one at **Chassepierre** has the most inspired the painters of the Gaume. Hidden in a steep-sided gorge, the village needs to be seen from above. From here the slate roofs blend harmoniously with the Romanesque Saint Martin Church, to which was added, in 1702, a bulbous baroque bell-tower.

Von allen Landschaften zwischen der Semois und der Vierre haben **Chassepierre** und Umgebung am häufigsten Maler aus dem äußersten Süden Belgiens zu Werken angeregt. Man sollte sich das in einer Schlucht eingeklemmte Dorf von oben ansehen. Dann sind die Schieferdächer völlig im Einklang mit der romanischen Sankt-Martinskirche, die 1702 mit einem barocken Zwiebelturm ausgestattet wurde.

◁

Rivière fantasque, se contorsionnant en replis infinis, la Semois parcourt une terre de légende, peuplée de fées et de nutons. Le long de ses rives, les villages alignent leurs maisons sur des terrasses de rochers. Les fermes y sont souvent d'anciens manoirs, comme à **Dohan** (1619).

De Semois is een grillige rivier die zich in talloze bochten wringt, en door een streek stroomt die rijk is aan legenden vol feeën en kabouterachtige "nutons". Langs de oevers liggen de dorpen en kijken de vaak op rotsterrassen gebouwde huizen op de rivier neer. Zoals hier in **Dohan** waren veel boerderijen kasteeltjes (1619).

The capricious, serpentine Semois river coils its tortuous way through a land of legend, peopled by fairies and gnomes. Villages built on rocky terraces dominate its banks. Farms such as that at **Dohan**, built in 1619, are often old manors.

Die grillenhafte Semois windet und krümmt sich wie eine Schlange, während sie durch eine Gegend strömt, in der — so sagt es die Legende — Feen und Kobolde ihr Wesen bzw. Unwesen treiben. Die Ufer entlang strecken sich die Dörfer aus und die oft auf felsigen Vorsprüngen gebauten Häuser schauen auf den Fluss hinab. Wie in **Dohan** (1619) sind manche Bauernhöfe erhalten gebliebene Schlösschen.

▷

À **Vresse**, au confluent de la Semois et du ruisseau de Petit-Fays, un pont à trois arches irrégulières pourrait avoir été construit à l'époque romaine. En 1774, après une violente crue dont la rivière était coutumière, il a été reconstruit par la fabrique de l'église Saint-Lambert d'où son nom de pont Saint-Lambert. Les parapets qui bordent le tablier en dos d'âne furent alors recouverts de lourdes dalles de schiste.

Vresse, gelegen aan de samenvloeiing van de Semois en de beek de Petit-Fays, heeft een brug met drie ongelijkmatige bogen die zou kunnen dateren uit de Romeinse periode. In 1744, nadat het water van de rivier naar gewoonte plots fel was gestegen, moest de brug heropgebouwd worden. Dit gebeurde met de hulp van de kerkfabriek van Saint-Lambert, vanwaar de huidige naam van de brug : pont Saint-Lambert. De relingen aan weerskanten van het sterk gewelfde bruggedek werden toen bedekt met zware leistenen.

At **Vresse** where the Petit-Fays brook joins the Semois there is a bridge with three irregular arches which looks like it could have built in Roman times. It was rebuilt by the works office of Saint Lambert's church in 1774 after a flood of more than usual violence, whence its name, Saint Lambert's bridge. The parapets bordering the way of the hump-backed bridge were recovered with heavy schist flagstone at that time.

In **Vresse**, wo die Semois und der Petit-Fays-Bach zusammenfließen, gibt es eine mit drei unregelmäßigen Bögen versehene Brücke, die noch aus der Römerzeit stammen könnte. Im Jahre 1774 wurde die Brücke nach starkem Hochwasser, das für den Fluss charakteristisch war, durch den Kirchenrat der St. Lambertuskirche wieder aufgebaut. Deshalb trägt die Brücke heute den Namen St. Lambertusbrücke. Die Brüstung, die den Grat bildenden Brückenbelag säumt, wurde dabei mit schweren Schieferplatten bedeckt.

Des hauteurs de Botassart, l'on découvre un fabuleux spectacle : le **Tombeau du Géant**, presqu'île boisée enserrée par la Semois, au centre d'un « gouffre immense de verdure où la forêt déferle jusqu'au plus lointain horizon... dans une solitude absolue, parmi les remous des crêtes ».

Vanaf de hoogten van Botassart ziet men een adembenemend schouwspel : het **Graf van de Reus**, een bomenrijk schiereiland, omstroomd door de Semois, temidden van « een geweldige groene kloof, waar het woud zich tot aan de einder ontrolt, in een volmaakte eenzaamheid, tussen de welvende heuvelkammen ».

From the heights of Botassart, the visitor has a particularly impressive view of the **Giant's Tomb**, a wooded peninsula enclosed by the Semois, amid « a vast green chasm, with forest reaching to the furthermost horizon... in perfect solitude, among the undulating crests ».

Von den Höhen von Botassart aus bietet sich dem Besucher ein fabelhaftes Schauspiel: das sogenannte **Grab des Riesen**, eine von der Semois einge-schlossene bewaldete Halbinsel inmitten eines "riesigen grünen Abgrundes, wo sich der Wald bis zum fernsten Horizont ausbreitet... in einer absoluten Einsam-keit, auf den Hängen der Gebirgsrücken".

Longue rue de quatre kilomètres, jalonnée par la collégiale gothique et dominée par la forteresse, **Dinant** a oublié le temps où elle faisait trembler ses voisins. Elle se contente de défier les mâchoires de ses visiteurs en leur offrant ses fameuses *couques au miel*, de formes variées.

Met zijn 4 km lange straat waaraan de collegiale kerk in gotische stijl is gelegen en beschermd door zijn vesting, was **Dinant** eens de schrik van de naburige steden. De enige uitdaging die de bezoekers nu nog moeten trotseren, bestaat in het bijten van de befaamde honingkoeken van uiteenlopende vorm.

Dinant consists chiefly of a long street, almost four kilometers long, enhanced by the Gothic collegiate church and dominated by the fortress. Dinant has forgotten the times when it awed its neighbours, being content nowadays to challenge the visitors' teeth with its honey cakes which are baked in a host of different shapes.

Dinant besteht aus einer vier Kilometer langen Straße, an der eine gotische Stiftskiche steht, die von einer Festung überragt wird. Die Stadt hat die Zeiten vergessen, in denen die Nachbarn vor ihr zitterten. Heute begnügt sich Dinant damit, die Kinnbacken seiner Besucher auf die Probe zu stellen, indem es ihnen seine bekannten Honigkuchen verschiedener Form anbietet.

△

Dédiée à saint Hadelin, l'église de **Celles** (XIᵉ siècle) est un type remarquable de sanctuaire roman rural. Elle repose sur deux cryptes et deux tourelles d'escalier flanquent le clocher massif.

De kerk van **Celles** (11de eeuw), gewijd aan Sint Hadelinus, is een merkwaardig type van landelijk-romaanse kerkbouw. Het gebouw rust op twee onderaardse gewelven en twee traptorentjes klimmen naast de massieve klokkentoren omhoog.

Dedicated to Saint Hadelin, the 11th century church of **Celles** is an outstanding example of the rural Romanesque sanctuary. It has two crypts and the massive bell-tower is flanked with two stair turrets.

Die dem heiligen Hadelin geweihte Kirche in **Celles** (11. Jh.) ist ein bemerkenswertes Beispiel romanischer Dorfkirchen. Sie ruht auf zwei Krypten, und zwei Treppentürme flankieren den massiven Glockenturm.

▷

Reconstruit en 1622 autour d'un robuste donjon du XIIIᵉ siècle qui a résisté à tous les assauts, le **château de Spontin** a gardé son aspect défensif moyenâgeux. Le pont-levis franchit toujours les eaux limpides du Bocq qui remplissent les douves.

De **burcht van Spontin** werd in 1622 herbouwd rond een robuuste vestingtoren uit de 13de eeuw die alle aanvallen had weerstaan. Het kasteel behield zijn middeleeuws, defensief karakter volkomen. De ophaalbrug weerspiegelt zich nog immer in het water van de Bocq dat de slotgracht vult.

Reconstructed in 1622 around a robust 13th century keep that had resisted every assault, the **castle of Spontin** has retained its defensive mediæval character. The drawbridge still spans the clear waters of the river Bocq which serves as the moat.

Die 1622 rund herum um einen starken Wachtturm aus dem 13. Jh., der alle Angriffe überstand, wiederaufgebaute **Burg Spontin** behielt ihr mittelalterliches Gesicht. Die Zugbrücke überragt noch immer die klaren Gewässer des Bocq, der die Wassergräben füllt.

◁

Charles-Alexis de Montpellier, seigneur d'**Annevoie**, avait la nostalgie de Versailles et la passion des jardins à la française. Au XVIIIᵉ siècle il construisit une demeure de style classique à côté d'une vieille tour privilégiaire du XVᵉ siècle. Davantage encore que le château, les jardins fleuris, les charmilles bien taillées et les frondaisons romantiques font la renommée d'Annevoie.

Charles-Alexis de Montpellier, heer van **Annevoie**, trachtte het ideaal van Versailles en de Franse tuinarchitectuur na te streven. In de 18de eeuw bouwde hij een woning in klassieke stijl naast een oude, als privilege toegekende toren uit de 15de eeuw. Meer nog dan het kasteel dragen de tuinen vol bloemperken, de keurig gesnoeide heggen en lieflijke boomgroepen bij tot de roem van Annevoie.

Charles-Alexis de Montpellier, the lord of **Annevoie**, had a passion for Versailles and for formal French gardens. In the 18th century he built a classical mansion next to an old 15th century tower. But Annevoie is known particularly for its flower-gardens, well-trimmed arbours, and romantic greenery.

Charles-Alexis de Montpellier, Herr auf **Annevoie**, schwärmte für Versailles und Gärten im französischen Stil. Im 18. Jh. baute er neben einem alten Turm aus dem 15. Jh. einen Wohnsitz im klassischen Stil. Mehr noch als dem Schloss verdankt Annevoie seinen blumenreichen Gärten, beschnittenen Laubengängen und romantischen Gartenanlagen seinen Ruf.

▷

Toen Europa nog niet doorsneden werd door autosnelwegen, verbleef een deel van de gegoede burgerij 's zomers in hun landgoed aan de oevers van de Maas. Sommige van die verblijven hadden een torentje, een teken van de sociale rang van de eigenaars. **Van Jambes tot Yvoir**, langs Dave en zijn eiland, staan woningen met een voorkomen van kleine kasteeltjes. Ze dateren uit de 19de en 20ste eeuw en staan aan de oevers van de Maas of tussen de rivier en de rotsachtige hellingen.

Au temps ou l'Europe n'était pas encore striée d'autoroutes, une partie de la grande bourgeoisie s'en allait passer la belle saison en ses maisons de campagne sur les rives de la Meuse. Certaines étaient dotées d'une tourelle, significative du rang social de leur propriétaire. **De Jambes à Yvoir**, en passant par Dave et son île, les demeures aux allures de petits castels de la fin du XIXᵉ et du début du XXᵉ siècle bordent la Meuse ou s'étagent entre celle-ci et les falaises rocheuses.

At the time when Europe was not yet criss-crossed by autoroutes many of the wealthy middle-class spent their summers in country houses, some of which had turrets signifying the social position of the owner, on the banks of the Meuse. **From Jambes to Yvoir**, passing by Dave and its islet, these miniature mansions of the late 19th and early 20th centuries line the banks of the river or perch between it and the rocky cliffs.

Früher, als Europa noch nicht von einem Autobahnnetz durchzogen war, verbrachte ein Teil des Großbürgertums die schöne Jahreszeit in Landhäusern am Ufer der Maas. Einige der Häuser besaßen ein Erkertürmchen, das auf den sozialen Stand des Besitzers schließen liess. **Vom Jambes bis Yvoir**, vorbei an Dave und seiner Insel, säumen die Wohnsitze im Stile von kleinen Schlössern aus dem 19. und Anfang des 20. Jhs. Die Maas oder reihen sich terrassenartig von deren Ufer bis zu den Klippen.

◁

Le corps de logis, les tours et les tourelles du château de **Walzin** (XIIIᵉ siècle), restauré en 1932, semblent le prolongement naturel de la muraille rocheuse qui se dresse à pic le long de la Lesse.

Het hoofdgebouw, de torens en de torentjes van het kasteel **Walzin** (13de eeuw) zijn in 1932 gerestaureerd, maar lijken de natuurlijke voortzetting van de rotsachtige, steile boorden van de Lesse.

The main wing, towers and turrets of the castle of **Walzin** (13th century), which was restored in 1932, seem to be a natural extension of the sheer rockface rising from the river Lesse.

Der Hauptbau, die Türme und Türmchen des Schlosses **Walzin** (13. Jh.), das 1932 restauriert wurde, scheinen die natürliche Verlängerung der Felswand zu sein, die sich senkrecht längs der Lesse erhebt.

▷▷

Descendant tumultueusement de Falmignoul, les eaux du Colébi creusèrent jadis une impressionnante série de marmites dans les masses rocheuses qui surplombent la rive droite de la Meuse. Ces gorges sauvages enchantent les alpinistes qui escaladent les **rochers de Freyr**. Au pied de la pente plus douce de l'autre rive, le château se laisse escorter par des jardins géométriques, dessinés en 1760 dans le style de Le Nôtre. L'aile qui longe le fleuve date de 1571.

Tijdens haar luidruchtige afdaling van Falmignoul groef de Colébi eertijds een indrukwekkende reeks uithollingen in de rotsmassa op de rechteroever van de Maas. Deze woeste engten zijn een trekpleister voor bergklimmers die de **muur van Freyr** opklauteren. Aan de voet van de zachte helling op de andere oever ligt het kasteel, omgeven door in 1760 in Le Nôtre-stijl getekende tuinen. De vleugel langs de rivier dateert van 1571.

In their tumultuous descent from Falmignoul, the waters of the Colébi have carved out an impressive series of potholes in the giant rocks overlooking the West bank of the Meuse. These wild gorges have become one of the favourite haunts of rockclimbers. On the opposite riverbank, where the slope is not so steep, **Freyr** Castle stands in the midst of lovely gardens of geometric design, laid out in the style of Le Nôtre. The wing closest to the river dates from 1571.

Einstmals gruben die von Falmignoul herabstürzenden Wasser des Colébi eine eindrucksvolle Reihe von Kesseln in die Felsenmassen, die das rechte Ufer der Maas überragen. Diese wilden Schluchten begeistern die Bergsteiger, die auf die **Freyrfelsen** klettern. Am Fuße des sanfteren Abhangs auf dem gegenüberliegenden Ufer liegt das Schloss mit seinen 1760 im Le Nôtre-Stil gezeichneten geometrischen Gärten. Der Schlossflügel längs des Stromes stammt aus dem Jahre 1571.

◁

Les églises de style classique n'abondent pas en Belgique. L'une des plus belles, tout en gardant un mouvement baroque, est incontestablement la **cathédrale Saint-Aubain de Namur**, édifiée de 1751 à 1763 selon les plans de l'architecte italien Gaetano Pizzoni. L'emplacement du dôme, à la croisée du transept, et la puissance des colonnes qui rythment les travées assurent une grande noblesse à l'édifice.

De classicistische kerken in België zijn haast op de vingers van één hand te tellen. De **St-Aubain kathedraal te Namen** is één der mooiste, al merkt men er nog een naklank van barokke onstuimigheid. Ze werd tussen 1751 en 1763 volgens plannen van de Italiaan Gaetano Pizzoni gebouwd. De koepel boven de viering van deze kruiskerk en de kloeke pilaren, die het ritme van de binnenruimte bepalen, wekken een indruk van verhevenheid en plechtstatigheid.

There are not many churches in the classical style in Belgium and one of the most handsome, though with minor baroque elements, is undoubtedly the **cathedral of Namur**. Saint Aubain was built between 1751 and 1763 following the plans of an Italian architect, Gaetano Pizzoni. The dome placed on the transept crossing and the powerful columns delineating the bays give a great nobility to the building.

In Belgien gibt es nur sehr wenige Kirchen in klassizistischem Stil. Die **Kathedrale St.-Aubain in Namur**, in der die barocke Ungestümtheit gewissermaßen noch nachschwingt, ist eine der schönsten. Sie wurde von 1751 bis 1763 nach Plänen des Italieners Gaetano Pizzoni errichtet. Die Kuppel über der Vierung und die wuchtigen, in rhythmischer Hinsicht wirkungsvollen Pfeiler strahlen erhabene Größe aus.

(Page suivante)
Le style Louis XV domine l'aménagement intérieur de la **maison de Groesbeeck-de Croix à Namur** reconstruit de 1750 à 1760, mais avec de fréquents rappels des formes régionales, notamment pour les cheminées. Devenu propriété de la ville, il est depuis 1935 un musée d'arts décoratifs. L'un des plus riches de Wallonie mais, surtout, un musée où meubles précieux, horloges, porcelaines de Chine et autres objets d'art du XVIIIᵉ siècle bénéficient d'un décor de cette époque parfaitement conservé.

(Volgende bladzijde)
Het **huis de Groesbeeck-de Croix te Namen** werd tussen 1750 en 1760 heropgebouwd. Hoewel in het interieur de Lodewijk-XV-stijl duidelijk overheerst, wordt ook vaak herinnerd aan streekgebonden vormen, bijvoorbeeld bij de schoorstenen. De stad verwierf het huis in 1935 en bracht er een museum voor schone kunsten in onder. Het is één van de meest uitgebreide van Wallonië. Maar bovenal is het een museum waar kostbare meubelen, klokken, Chinees porselein en andere kunstvoorwerpen uit de 18de eeuw worden tentoongesteld in een decor dat de tijdsgeest perfect heeft bewaard.

(Next page)
The interior decoration of the **Groesbeeck-de Croix Mansion in Namur**, rebuilt from 1750 to 1760, is dominated by the Louis XV style but with many references to regional styles such as in the fireplaces. Acquired by the city, it has been a Museum of Decorative Arts since 1935, one of the richest in Wallonia. In this museum precious furniture, clocks, Chinese porcelain and other 18th century art objects benefit from the perfectly preserved original decor

(Folgende Seite)
Zwar überwiegt bei der Inneneinrichtung des **Groesbeek-de Croix-Hauses in Namur**, das zwischen 1750 und 1760 wieder aufgebaut wurde, das Louis-quinze, aber oft — besonders bei den Kaminen — sind auch regionale Ausprägungen zu beobachten. Das Gebäude, das sich im Besitz der Stadt befindet, ist seit 1935 ein Museum für Kunstgewerbe. Es gehört in Wallonien zu denen, die die kostbarsten Schätze ausstellen, ist aber vor allem ein Museum, in dem wertvolle Möbel, Uhren, Porzellan und andere Objekte des 18. Jh. in einem einzigartig erhaltenen Dekor dieser Epoche zu sehen sind.

△
Les sept volumineuses tours en grès ferrugineux de **Corroy-le-Château** faisaient partie de la ligne de défense du Duché de Brabant. Après les Vianden qui l'édifièrent vers 1270, la forteresse fut détenue par les Nassau du XVᵉ au XIXᵉ siècle. Par alliance, il passa aux Trazegnies qui l'occupent encore. Le pont de pierre qui enjambe les douves mène à une barbacane. Le pont-levis a disparu, remplacé par un passage vers le puissant châtelet d'entrée flanqué de deux tours semi-circulaires reliées entre elles par une courtine.

De zeven omvangrijke torens in ijzerhoudende zandsteen van **Corroy-le-Château** maakten deel uit van de verdedigingslijn van het hertogdom Brabant. De versterkte burcht werd rond 1270 opgetrokken door de familie Vianden. Van de 15de tot de 19de eeuw was ze in handen van het geslacht Nassau. Door familiebanden ging het over naar de Trazegnies, die haar ook nu nog bewonen. De stenen brug die de slotgracht overspant eindigt op een ravelijn. De ophaalbrug is verdwenen en werd vervangen door een toegang tot het aanzienlijke ingangskasteeltje, geflankeerd door twee halfronde torens die met elkaar verbonden zijn door een courtine.

The seven large towers in reddish-brown sandstone of **Corroy-le-Château** were part of the defensive line of the Duchy of Brabant. The Vianden family built it around 1270 and then it was held from the 15th to 19th centuries by the House of Nassau. It passed by marriage to the Trazegnies who still live there. The stone bridge over the defensive ditch leads to a barbican. The drawbridge has disappeared, replaced by a passageway to the sturdy fortified gate house flanked by two semi-circular towers linked by a curtain wall.

Die sieben gewaltigen aus Eisensandstein errichteten Türme des **Schlosses von Corroy** waren Bestandteil der Verteidigungslinie des Brabanter Herzogtums. Nach der Familie Vianden, die die Festung um 1270 erbaute, wurde sie vom 15. bis zum 19. Jahrhundert von der Familie Nassau unterhalten, ehe das Schloss durch Heirat an die Familie Trazegnies überging, in deren Besitz es sich heute noch befindet. Die Steinbrücke, die den Burggraben überspannt, führt zu einer Barbakane. Die Zugbrücke wurde durch einen Durchgang zum mächtigen Eingangsgebäude ersetzt, an das sich beidseitig zwei halbrunde Türme anschließen, die wiederum durch eine Kurtine miteinander verbunden sind.

Peu après l'ouverture de la Grand-Place de **Mons**, l'hôtel de ville y fut édifié entre 1458 et 1467 mais il s'effondra partiellement dix ans plus tard. Le Magistrat fit alors appel au célèbre architecte brabançon Mathieu de Layens qui avait construit l'hôtel de ville de Louvain. Aussi les deux niveaux de la façade sont-ils largement inspirés du gothique brabançon, tout comme l'ornementation flamboyante au-dessus des fenêtres.

The City Hall of **Mons** was built between 1458 and 1467 shortly after the Grand-Place was laid out but part of it collapsed ten years later. The Magistrate then engaged the famous architect Mathieu de Layens of Brabant who had built Louvain's city hall. Thus, the two levels of the façade are greatly influenced by Brabant Gothic as is the Flamboyant detailing above the windows.

Kort na de opening van de grote markt van **Bergen** werd daar tussen 1458 en 1467 het stadhuis gebouwd, dat 10 jaar later reeds gedeeltelijk instortte. De magistraat deed toen een beroep op de beroemde Brabantse architect Mattheus de Laeyens, die het stadhuis van Leuven had ontworpen. Zowel de twee verdiepingen tellende gevel als de flamboyante versieringen boven de vensters getuigen van de invloeden van de Brabantse gotiek.

Kurze Zeit nach Eröffnung des Marktplatzes von **Mons** wurde das Rathaus dort zwischen 1458 und 1467 errichtet, stürzte jedoch zehn Jahre darauf teilweise wieder ein. Der Magistrat beauftragte daraufhin den berühmten Brabanter Baumeister Mathieu de Layens, der das Löwener Rathaus erbaut hatte. Die beiden Etagen der Fassade sind ebenso wie die spätgotische Verzierung unter den Fenstern weitgehend von der Brabanter Gotik beeinflusst worden.

D'imposantes grilles en fer forgé s'ouvrent sur la cour d'honneur du **château de Seneffe**. L'édifice a été construit de 1763 à 1768 pour Julien Depestre, que l'on considérait comme le principal homme d'affaires des Pays-Bas autrichiens. L'architecte s'inspira du château que Vanvitelli édifia pour le roi de Naples; il en résulte un style Louis XV proche de l'Antiquité. Laissé à l'abandon par ses propriétaires successifs, le château fut sauvé de justesse par le Ministère de la Culture française. Seneffe abrite aujourd'hui un musée de l'argenterie.

Imposing wrought-iron gates open onto the main courtyard of the **château of Seneffe**. The mansion was built between 1763 and 1768 for Julien Depestre, at that time the principal businessman of the Austrian Low Countries. The architect was inspired by a château designed by Vanvitelli for the King of Naples. The result is a Louis XV style building with heavy Antique overtones. Abandoned by suceeding owners, the building was saved from ruin at the last minute by the Ministry of Culture of the French Community. Seneffe now houses a Silver Museum.

Indrukwekkende smeedijzeren hekken geven uit op het voorplein van het **kasteel van Seneffe**. Het gebouw werd opgetrokken tussen 1763 en 1768 voor Julien Depestre, één van de belangrijkste zakenmannen der Oostenrijkse Nederlanden. De architect inspireerde zich bij het maken van de plannen op het kasteel dat Vanvitelli bouwde voor de koning van Napels. Het resultaat was een Lodewijk XV-stijl die dicht aanleunt bij de Oudheid. De opeenvolgende eigenaars lieten het kasteel verkommeren tot het werd gered door het Ministerie van Cultuur van de Franse Gemeenschap. Seneffe biedt nu onderdak aan een zilvermuseum.

Imposante schmiedeeiserne Gitter mit vergoldeten Abschlüssen führen auf den Hof des **Schlosses von Seneffe**. Das Gebäude entstand von 1763 bis 1768 für Julien Depestre, der als die wichtigste Person in der Geschäftswelt der österreichischen Niederlande galt. Der Architekt ließ sich bei seinen Plänen von dem Schloss, das Vanvitelli für den König von Neapel errichtete, inspirieren. Das Resultat ist ein Louis-quinze-Stil, der an die Antike erinnert, inspirieren. Das Schloss, das unter den aufeinanderfolgenden Besitzern in einen immer verwahrlosteren Zustand geriet, konnte gerade noch vom Ministerium für französische Kultur gerettet werden. Seneffe beherbergt heute ein Museum für Silberwaren.

Au bout d'une longue allée de hêtres deux fois séculaires, le château princier de **Belœil** a gardé sa forme primitive de quadrilatère irrégulier. L'intérieur raconte les fastes des princes de Ligne et abrite des collections inestimables. Et dans les jardins où la fantaisie l'emporte souvent sur l'ordonnance classique, on ne s'étonnerait pas de rencontrer le feldmaréchal Charles-Joseph de Ligne, le diplomate le plus spirituel du siècle le plus léger.
(Ci-dessus)
Ouvert sur le vestibule du château de Belœil, le salon des Maréchaux s'apparente à une salle de musée. Des boiseries aux armes de Claude-Lamoral II de Ligne encadrent des tapisseries de Beauvais.

Aan het einde van een meer dan 200 jaar oude beukenlaan ligt het kasteel **Belœil**, met zijn oorspronkelijke plattegrond van een onregelmatige vierhoek. Binnen herleeft de pracht en praal van de prinsen de Ligne. Er zijn vele voorwerpen van onschatbare waarde te bezichtigen. In de tuinen, waar de fantasie dikwijls de overhand heeft op de klassieke orde, zou men haast verwachten plots veldmaarschalk Charles-Joseph de Ligne tegen te komen, de geestigste aller diplomaten uit het lichtzinnigste tijdperk der geschiedenis.
(Hierboven)
De vlak naast de vestibule van het kasteel van Belœil gelegen ontvangzaal der maarschalken heeft het voorkomen van een museumzaal. Aan weerskanten van de wandtapijten uit Beauvais prijkt het blazoen van Claude-Lamoral II de Ligne op de lambrizering.

Standing at the end of a long avenue of bicentenarian beeches, the princely castle of **Belœil** has retained its original lay-out in the shape of an irregular square. The castle contains mementos of the de Ligne Princes as well as invaluable works of art. In the grounds, imagination often triumphs over classical design, a fitting setting for Field-Marshal Charles-Joseph de Ligne, the wittiest diplomat of the most lighthearted century.
(Above)
The Marshals' Salon, opening off the vestibule of Belœil castle, is like a museum. Panelling bearing the arms of Claude-Lamoral II de Ligne frames Beauvais tapestries.

Am Ende einer langen, zweihundertjährigen Buchenallee hat das Fürstenschloss **Belœil** seine ursprüngliche, unregelmäßige Viereckform behalten. Das Innere erzählt die Ruhmestaten der Fürsten von Ligne und beherbergt unschätzbare Sammlungen. In den Gärten, in denen die Phantasie die klassische Anordnung oft übertrifft, würde man sich nicht wundern, den Feldmarschall Karl-Joseph von Ligne, den geistreichsten Diplomaten des leichtfertigsten Jahrhunderts, zu treffen.
(Oben)
Der Empfangssaal der Marschälle im Schloss von Belœil liegt gleich neben der Vorhalle und sieht aus wie ein Museum. Die mit dem Wappen Claude-Lamorals II. geschmückte Holzverkleidung umrahmt die Wandteppiche aus Beauvais.

Érigé en 1752 par François-Philippe Freneau, comte de Gomegnies, le château d'**Attre** offre une façade sobre, de goût français, entre deux pavillons de style Louis XVI. Une large pelouse a remplacé l'ancienne cour pavée où, les jours de grande réception, piaffaient les chevaux des carrosses.

La décoration intérieure d'Attre fut achevée par le fils du constructeur, François-Ferdinand qui fut chambellan de l'empereur Joseph II. Sur les murs du salon de réception, les trophées en relief alternent avec les peintures attribuées à Hubert Robert. Le mobilier est d'époque, tout comme la cheminée Louis XV en marbre de Rance.

Het in 1752 door Frans-Filips Freneau, graaf van Gomegnies, gebouwde kasteel van **Attre** bestaat uit een hoofdgebouw in sobere Franse stijl tussen twee Lodewijk-XVI-paviljoens. De vroeger geplaveide binnenplaats, waarop de paarden toen ter gelegenheid van grote recepties stonden te trappelen, is nu door een uitgestrekt grasperk vervangen.

De binnenhuisdecoratie van Attre werd pas voltooid ten tijde van Frans-Ferdinand, zoon van Frans-Filips en kamerheer van keizer Jozef II. Op de muren prijken trofeeën met verheven beeldwerk en aan H. Robert toegeschreven schilderijen. De meubels zijn 18de-eeuws net zoals het uit Rance komende marmer van de schouw in Lodewijk-XV-stijl.

Built in 1752 by François-Philippe Freneau, Count de Gomegnies, **Attre** château presents a restrained French style façade flanked by two Louis XVI pavilions. A large lawn has replaced the old paved court-yard where carriage horses once stamped and snorted.

The interior decoration of Attre was completed by the builder's son, François-Ferdinand, chamberlain to Emperor Joseph II. Trophies in relief alternate with paintings attributed to Hubert Robert in the main drawing room. The furniture is of the period as is the Louis XV mantelpiece in Rance marble.

Das 1752 in französischem Stil von F.-Ph. Freneau, Graf von Gomegnies, gebaute Schloss von **Attre** besteht aus einem fast schmucklosen Hauptgebäude nach französischem Muster zwischen vorgezogenen Pavillons im Louis-seize. Der früher gepflasterte Hof, auf dem die Gespanne bei festlichen Empfängen anzufahren pflegten, wurde in eine große Rasenfläche umgewandelt.

Franz-Ferdinand, dem Sohn des Bau- und Kammerherrn Kaiser Josephs II., verdankt Attre die Vollendung seiner Innenausstattung. Trophäen mit erhabener Arbeit sowie H. Robert zugeschriebene Gemälde schmücken die Empfangsräume. Die Möbel und der mit Marmor aus Rance ausgelegte Kamin im Louis-quinze sind ebenfalls aus dem 18. Jh.

(Double page suivante)
Tournai partage avec Tongres le titre de plus ancienne ville de Belgique. Vers 275, la construction de la chaussée romaine unissant le Rhin à la mer du Nord lui permit de contrôler un faisceau de routes. Lorsque, vers 431, les Francs saliens déferlèrent sur la région, Clodion s'installa dans la cité scaldéenne. Ce fut l'origine d'une des trois dynasties de France.

Entre 1110 et 1141 commença la construction de la cathédrale. Sommet de l'architecture romane, Notre-Dame frappe d'abord par le puissant faisceau des cinq tours, qui couronne la croisée du transept.

Quant au plus ancien beffroi belge, érigé à la fin du XIIᵉ siècle mais souvent remanié, il semble défier la cathédrale.

(Next two pages)
Tournai shares with Tongeren the title of the oldest city of Belgium. Construction of the Roman road linking the Rhine to the North Sea in 275 gave it control of a web of routes. When the Salian Franks invaded the region in 431, Clodion set up his court in the Scaldian city, founding one of the three dynasties of France.

Construction of the cathedral began between 1110 and 1141. Notre-Dame, one of the jewels of Romanesque architecture, impresses the viewer first of all by the powerful grouping of its five towers, crowning the transept crossing.

Built at the end of the 12th century, but often remodelled, the oldest belfry in Belgium seems to challenge the cathedral.

(Volgende dubbele bladzijde)
Samen met Tongeren is **Doornik** de oudste stad van België. De aanleg van een Romeinse heirbaan tussen Rijn en Noordzee rond 275 bracht met zich mee dat Doornik een knooppunt in een ingewikkeld verkeersnet werd. Toen omstreeks 431 de Saliërs de streek veroverden, vestigde Chlodio zich in de Scheldestad. Zo werd de stad de bakermat van één der Franse vorstenhuizen.

Tussen 1110 en 1141 begon de bouw van de O.-L.Vrouwekathedraal, één van de hoogtepunten van de Romaanse bouwkunst. Wat vooral opvalt, is de bundel gevormd door de vijf massale torens die viering en dwarsbeuk bekronen.

In de buurt staat, bijna uitdagend, het oudste belfort van België. Het werd op het einde van de 12de eeuw opgetrokken maar herhaaldelijk herbouwd.

(Nächste Doppelseite)
Tournai ist gemeinsam mit Tongeren die älteste Stadt Belgiens. Der Bau einer römischen Heerstraße zwischen Rhein und Nordsee um 275 machte Tournai zu einem wichtigen Verkehrsknotenpunkt. Als die salischen Franken um 431 das Gebiet überrannten, wählte Chlodio die Stadt als Regierungssitz. So wurde sie die Wiege eines der französischen Herrschergeschlechter.

Zwischen 1110 und 1141 begann der Bau der Liebfrauenkirche, eines der Juwelen der romanischen Baukunst. Die fünf wuchtigen Vierecktürme, welche die Vierung von Lang- und Querhaus krönen bzw. umschließen, sind äußerst eindrucksvoll.

Der im 12. Jh. entstandene, oft umgebaute älteste Bergfried Belgiens steht fast herausfordernd der Kathedrale gegenüber.

△

Het standbeeld van Dirk Martens, in 1473 de eerste boekdrukker in België, staat voor het schepenhuis en het belfort (15de eeuw) van **Aalst**, Martens' geboortestad. Op de plaats van het Vleeshuis werd in 1630-1634 een weeshuis in Vlaamse renaissancestijl opgetrokken met vier barokke topgevels en beneden een uit elf arcaden bestaande open galerij. Daarna kreeg het de naam *Beurs van Amsterdam* en was het een herberg.

La statue de Thierry Martens, premier imprimeur belge en 1473, a été érigée devant la maison échevinale et le beffroi (XVᵉ siècle) d'**Alost**, sa ville natale. À l'emplacement de la halle aux viandes s'édifia en 1630-1634 un orphelinat qui conjuguait le style Renaissance flamande de l'arcade à onze travées avec le style baroque des quatre pignons. Il devint ensuite une auberge dont il a gardé le nom *Beurs van Amsterdam*.

This statue of Thierry Martens, the first Belgian printer in 1473, stands in front of the Council Chambers and belfry (15th century) at **Aalst**, his native town. After the Butchers Hall was demolished an orphanage was built on the site between 1630 and 1634. The building combines the Flemish Renaissance style of the eleven-bayed arcade with the baroque style of the four gables. If then became an inn to which it owes it present name of *Beurs van Amsterdam*.

Die Statue Thiery Martens', des ersten belgischen Druckers im Jahre 1473, wurde vor dem Schöffenhaus und dem Bergfried (15. Jh.) seiner Vaterstadt **Aalst** errichtet. Die Fleischhalle wurde 1630-1634 durch ein neugebautes Waisenhaus ersetzt. Die Arkadengalerie mit elf Traveen sowie der erste Stock sind in flämischem Renaissancestil gehalten; auf den vier völlig gleichen Giebelaufsätzen breiten sich geschwungene, barocke Formen aus. Später wurde daraus die «Börse von Amsterdam» genannte Gaststätte.

◁

De structuur en het overladen sierwerk van het **stadhuis van Oudenaarde** (1526-1537) behoren tot de flamboyante gotiek. Het uitspringende belfort bindt alle lijnen en vlakken van de gevel op gelukkige wijze samen. De opengewerkte koepel op de toren is bekroond met de keizerskroon van Karel V.

Par sa structure et son décor surabondant, l'**hôtel de ville d'Audenarde** (1526-1537) appartient au gothique flamboyant. Son beffroi en saillie unit avec bonheur toutes les lignes et tous les plans de la façade. Au sommet de la tour, une coupole ajourée représente la couronne impériale de Charles Quint.

By its structure and rich ornamentation, the **Town Hall of Oudenaarde** (1526-1537) belongs to the Flamboyant Gothic. The sweeping belfry has the happy effect of uniting all the lines and levels of the edifice. At the top of the spire, a openwork cupola represents the imperial crown of Charles the Fifth.

Mit seiner Struktur und seinen überreichen Verzierungen gehört das **Oudenaarder Rathaus** (1526-1537) zum spätgotischen Stil. Der vorgezogene Bergfried vereinigt in glücklicher Weise alle Linien und alle Ebenen. Auf der Turmspitze stellt eine durchbrochene Kuppel die Kaiserkrone Karls V. dar.

(Vorige drie blz.)

In **Gent**, langs de **Graslei**, staan het Romaanse *Koornstapelhuis* (1200), het kleine *Tolhuisje van de tolbaas* (1682), het *Korenmetershuis* (1698) en het gildenhuis der *Vrije Schippers* (1531); in één aanblik aanschouwt men vijf eeuwen bouwkunst.

(Hierboven)

Nummer 14 van de Graslei is het **gildenhuis van de Vrije Schippers**, dat in 1531 door de meester-metselaar Christoffel van den Berghe werd gebouwd. Op de overvloedig versierde voorgevel valt de glans der laatste vlammen van de flamboyante gotiek en die van het ochtendgloren van de Renaissance. Boven de poort bevindt zich een prachtig bas-reliëf waarop een kogge is uitgebeeld, één van die Baltische driemasters, die voor de van bedrijvigheid gonzende gildenhuizen ten anker lagen.

(Triple page précédente)

À **Gand**, au **Graslei** (quai aux Herbes), la maison romane de l'*Étape du blé* (1200), la menue logette du *Receveur de l'étape* (1682), la maison des *Mesureurs de grains* (1698) et celle cles *Francs Bateliers* (1531) font défiler cinq siècles d'architecture civile.

(Ci-dessus)

Au numéro 14 du quai aux Herbes, la **maison des Francs Bateliers** fut édifiée en 1531 par le maître maçon Christophe van den Berghe. Sa façade très ornée marie les dernières flammes du gothique flamboyant aux premières influences de la Renaissance. Le portail est surmonté d'un très beau bas-relief représentant un *cogge*, bateau à trois mâts de la Baltique, un de ceux qui s'amarraient devant les maisons corporatives débordantes d'activité.

(Preceding three pages)

In **Ghent**, on the **Graslei**, the Romanesque *Corn Granary* (1200), the diminutive lodge of the *Toll Collector* (1682), the *Grain Measurers house* (1698) and that of the *Free Boatmen* (1531) combine five centuries of secular architecture.

(Above)

At No. 14, Graslei, the **House of the Free Boatmen** was built in 1531 by the master mason Christophe van den Berghe. Its very ornate façade blends the last flickers of flamboyant Gothic with the first touches of Renaissance. The portal is topped by a beautiful low-relief representing a cog, a three-masted ship from the Baltic of the type that would tie up in front of the bustling guild houses.

(Vorausgehende drei S.)

In **Gent**, an der **Graslei** vertreten das romanische *Weizenstapelhaus* (1200), das kleine Häuschen des *Stapeleinnehmers* (1682), das *Kornmesserhaus* (1698) und das *Schifferhaus* (1531) fünf Jahrhunderte bürgerlicher Architektur.

(Oben)

Nummer 14 in der Graslei ist das **Haus der unabhängigen Schiffer**. Der Maurermeister Christoph van den Berghe baute es 1531. Auf die Fassade fallen der letzte Flammenglanz des Flamboyantstils und die ersten Strahlen der beginnenden Renaissance. Über dem Portal befindet sich ein sehr schönes Basrelief, auf dem man eine Kogge sieht, einen jener Dreimaster, die von der Ostsee kamen und vor den Gildehäusern voll bienenhafter Geschäftigkeit haltmachten.

In tegenstelling met de toren (1462-1534) van de **Sint-Baafs-kathe-draal**, die zijn spits in 1603 kwijtraakte, heeft het **belfort** (1313-1321) zijn weliswaar vaak omgebouwde en gerestaureerde top behouden. Wel hangt "Klokke Roeland" er niet meer om de poorters ten strijde te roepen en liggen er in de geheimvolle kluizen van de benedenzaal geen keuren en handvesten meer opgeborgen maar de aan de pijl van de windwijzer vastgeklonken draak fonkelt en flikkert nog altijd boven Gent als een monster met gouden schubben.

Contrairement à la tour (1462-1534) de la **cathédrale Saint-Bavon**, qui perdit en 1603 la flèche qui la surmontait, celle du **beffroi** (1313-1321) en est encore pourvue. À son sommet, souvent remanié, «Klokke Roeland» n'appelle plus les Gantois à la révolte et il n'y a plus de privilège enfermé dans les coffres secrets de la salle inférieure. Mais, le ventre rivé sur la flèche, le dragon scintille toujours comme un monstre aux écailles d'or.

The **belfry** (1313-21), unlike the tower of **Saint Baaf's cathedral** (1462-1534) which lost its spire in 1603, still has its own. "Klokke Roeland" no longer urges citizens to rebellion from its often repaired summit, and privileges are no longer stored in the secret safes of the lower hall. However, the dragon, his belly pinned to the spire, still glitters like a gold scaled monster.

Im Gegensatz zum Turm (1462-1534) der **St.-Baafskathedrale**, die 1603 ihre Spitze verlor, ist die oft umgebaute Turmspitze des **Bergfrieds** (1313-1321) erhalten geblieben. Dort hängt jedoch keine „Klokke Roeland" mehr, um die Bürger zum Streit zu rufen, und in den geheimnisvollen Truhen des unteren Saales werden keine Privilegien mehr aufbewahrt. Doch, den Pfeil der Wetterfahne umklammernd, glänzt und funkelt der Drache noch immer über Gent wie ein mit goldenen Schuppen bedecktes Ungeheuer.

De hal van het **Groot Vleeshuis van Gent**, gebouwd van 1404 tot 1417, beslaat een volledige gevel van de Groentenmarkt. Het kon ganse kudden herbergen. Het binnenste heeft de ruimte van een kathedraal met stevige zuilen, terwijl de buitenkant door de onvermoeide herhaling van kleine gevels die zich in de Leie spiegelen, een legendarische atmosfeer schept.

Du Marché-aux-Légumes *(Groentenmarkt)*, la **Grande Boucherie de Gand** occupe tout un côté. Construite de 1404 à 1417, elle pouvait abriter des troupeaux entiers. L'intérieur a l'ampleur d'une cathédrale aux piliers puissants tandis que l'extérieur, par la répétition des petits pignons qui se mirent dans la Lys, crée une atmosphère de légende.

The **Great Butcher's Hall of Ghent** occupies the whole of one side of the Groentenmarkt. Built between the years 1404 and 1417, it could accommodate whole herds of cattle. The interior has the broad sweep of a pillared cathedral, while the endless repetition of minute gables reflected in the water of the Lys gives the exterior a legendary aspect.

Vom Gemüsemarkt *(Groentenmarkt)* nimmt die **große Fleischhalle von Gent** eine ganze Seite ein; sie wurde von 1404 bis 1417 erbaut und konnte ganze Herden fassen. Das Innere hat die Weite einer Kathedrale mit mächtigen Pfeilern, während das Äußere durch die unermüdliche Wiederholung der kleinen Giebel, die sich in der Leie spiegeln, eine Legendenstimmung schafft.

In Gent beleefden de gilden hun beste dagen vooral na 1302 en de over-winning van het volk op de patriciërs, die met de koning van Frankrijk samenspanden. Het mooie op één der hoeken van de Vrijdagmarkt gelegen pand was het gildenhuis van de leerlooiers (1451). Het heeft zijn naam **"Toreken"** natuurlijk te danken aan zijn sierlijke hoektoren die van 1483 dateert.

Les métiers gantois se sont surtout développés après l'année 1302 qui vit la victoire du peuple sur les patriciens alliés au roi de France. La corporation des Tanneurs avait sa maison (1451) admirablement située à un coin du Vrijdagmarkt (Marché du Vendredi). La jolie tourelle d'angle, dressée en 1483, lui a valu de s'appeler **« Het Toreken »**.

The guilds of Ghent developed swiftly after 1302 when the commoners triumphed over the patricians allied to the King of France. The Tanners Guild had its house (1451) well situated on a corner of the Vrijdagmarkt. The pretty corner turret, built in 1483, gave it the name **"Het Toreken"**.

Als das Volk 1302 seinen Sieg über die Patrizier davontrug, die mit dem König von Frankreich gemeinsame Sache machten, erreichten die Zünfte in Gent ihre höchste Blüte. An einer Ecke des Vrijdagmarkt steht das Haus der Lohgerber (1451), das dem 1483 hinzugefügten schmucken Turm seinen Namen **„Toreken"** (Türmchen) verdankt.

Van de drie vestingen, die in de Vlaamse vlakte de vooruitgeschoven verdediging vormden van Gent, is het kasteel van Wondelgem verdwenen, terwijl dat van **Ooidonk** mettertijd een lustoord is geworden. Alleen het kasteel van Laarne heeft zijn feodaal karakter uit de 11de eeuw bewaard. Het kasteel van Ooidonk werd gebouwd in de 14de eeuw. De naam ervan doet nog denken aan het moeras waarin het werd gebouwd. Het kasteel heeft nog de grootse allure van een herenwoning uit de 16de eeuw.

Des trois forteresses qui assuraient, dans la plaine flamande, la défense avancée de Gand, celle de Wondelgem a disparu et celle de **Ooidonk** a pris l'allure d'un castel de plaisance. Seul le château fort de Laarne a conservé le caractère féodal du XIe siècle. Le château de Ooidonk, dont le nom évoque le marais *(donk)* où il fut érigé au XIVe siècle, a gardé la grande allure d'une demeure seigneuriale du XVIe siècle.

Of the three fortresses in the Flemish plain which used to ensure the advanced defences of Ghent, the one at Wondelgem has disappeared entirely while that of **Ooidonk** has become a purely residential manorhouse. Only Laarne has retained its feudal 11th century character. The castle of Ooidonk, named after the marsh *(donk)* on which it was built in the 14th century, retains the stylish aspect of a 16th century manor-house.

Von den drei Burgen, die in der flandrischen Ebene die Verteidigung der Stadt Gent sicherten, ist Wondelgem verschwunden, und **Ooidonk** hat das Gesicht eines Lustschlosses angenommen. Allein Burg Laarne behielt ihr mittelalterliches Aussehen (11.Jh.). Schloss Ooidonk, dessen Name an das Moor erinnert, in dem es im 14. Jahrhundert errichtet wurde, hat das großartige Aussehen eines Herrensitzes aus dem 16. Jahrhundert bewahrt.

Naar verluidt heeft **Temse** zijn naam te danken aan Edward III, koning van Engeland, die in 1338 door de gelijkenis tussen de Scheldevallei en de oevers van de Theems zou zijn getroffen. Wat er ook van zij, het lot van deze bedrijvige industriestad werd in hoge mate bepaald door de Schelde die, naarmate ze de grens van Oost-Vlaanderen nadert, steeds breder wordt.

It is said that **Temse** owes its name to King Edward III of England who was struck by the similarity between the countryside of the Scheldt and that of the English river, the Thames. Be what may, the history of this industrious industrial town is intimately bound up with that of the river which broadens before leaving East Flanders.

On raconte que **Tamise** doit son nom au roi d'Angleterre Edouard III qui, en 1338, avait été frappé par la ressemblance du paysage scaldéen avec celui du fleuve anglais homonyme. Quoi qu'il en soit, l'histoire de cette ville industrielle et industrieuse se confond avec celle de l'Escaut qui a pris de l'ampleur avant de quitter la Flandre Orientale.

Die Legende führt den Namen der Stadt **Temse** auf den englischen König Eduard III. zurück, der sich 1338 über die verblüffende Ähnlichkeit zwischen dem Scheldetal bei Temse und dem der Themse gewundert haben soll. Wie dem auch sei, diese Industrie- und Handelsstadt verdankt der Schelde, die an der Grenze Ostflanderns immer breiter wird, ihren Wohlstand.

△

Op de voorgevel van het stadhuis van **Kaprijke** in het Meetjesland herinneren twee inscripties eraan dat het gebouw in 1663 werd opgetrokken, maar twintig jaar later in brand werd gestoken. Gelukkig slaagden de brandstichters — troepen van Lodewijk XIV — er slechts in het dak te beschadigen. Ook tijdens de restauratie-werkzaamheden in de 19de eeuw bleef de typisch landelijke barok-stijl onaangetast.

Deux inscriptions apposées sur la façade de la maison communa-le de **Kaprijke**, dans le Meetjesland, rappellent qu'elle fut construi-te en 1663 et incendiée vingt ans plus tard. Fort heureusement, lorsque les armées de Louis XIV y boutèrent le feu, elles ne réussi-rent qu'à endommager la toiture. La restauration du XIXe siècle ne modifia donc ni la structure ni la distinction de cet édifice de style baroque rural.

Two inscriptions on the façade of the town hall of **Kaprijke** in the Meetjesland state that it was built in 1663 and burned twenty years later. It is fortunate that when the soldiers of Louis XIV set it on fire only the roof was damaged. A nineteenth century restoration neither changed the structure nor spoiled the refinement of this building in the rural baroque style.

Auf der Fassade des Rathauses von **Kaprijke** im Meetjesland erinnern zwei Inschriften daran, dass das Gebäude 1663 errichtet und zwanzig Jahre danach in Brand gesteckt wurde. Zum Glück gelang es den Brandstiftern — Soldaten Ludwigs XIV. — nur, das Dach zu beschädigen. Der ländliche Barockstil des Gebäudes blieb wohl auch deshalb während der Restaurationsarbeiten im 19. Jh. völlig erhalten.

▷▷

Het **kasteel van Loppem** werd gebouwd tussen 1858 en 1862 en is een perfect voorbeeld van Vlaamse neo-gotiek. Tot in de kleinste details van zowel gevels als binnenafwerking verwees de architect naar het artistieke verleden van Vlaanderen.

Na afloop van de Eerste Wereldoorlog ontving koning Albert I er persoonlijkheden die hem informeerden over de toestand van het land. Deze discussies leidden tot de invoering van het algemeen stemrecht, zonder grondwetsherziening.

Exemple parfait du néo-gothique flamand, le **château de Loppem** fut bâti de 1858 à 1862. Jusqu'aux moindres détails des façades et de l'intérieur, l'architecte fit référence au passé artistique de la Flandre.

À l'issue de la Première Guerre mondiale, le roi Albert Ier y reçut des personnalités qui l'informèrent de la situation du pays. Discussions qui menèrent à l'instauration du suffrage universel sans révision constitutionnelle.

The **château of Loppem**, built 1858-63, is a perfect example of Flemish Gothic Revival. The architect has recalled the artistic past of Flanders down to the smallest detail of the exterior and interior.

After World War I King Albert I consulted here with prominent cit-izens who briefed him on problems facing the nation. These discus-sions led to granting universal male suffrage without resorting to constitutional reform.

Das **Schloss von Loppem**, ein ausgezeichnetes Beispiel flämischer Neugotik, wurde zwischen 1858 und 1862 erbaut. Bis in die geringsten Details der Fassaden und der Innenausstattung folgte der Architekt der künstlerischen Vergangenheit Flanderns.

Nach dem Ersten Weltkrieg empfing König Albert I. dort Persönlichkeiten, die ihn über die Lage des Landes informierten. Diese Diskussionen führten zur Einführung des allgemeinen Wahlrechts ohne Verfassungsänderung.

Brugge, de Rozenhoedkaai.
Bruges, le quai du Rosaire.
Bruges, the Rosary Wharf.
Brügge, der Rosenkranzkaai.

(*Hierboven*) Nadat ze Brugge doorlopen had, stroomde de Reie vroeger verder noordwaarts om in een zeearm uit te monden. Op die plaats kregen de oevers in de 13de eeuw de benaming Houtbrekersdam, omdat de scheepsbouwers er hun scheepshelling hadden gevestigd. Vandaag wordt de westelijke oever **Langerei** genoemd. Vanaf de Spiegelrei wordt ze geflankeerd door huizen in verschillende stijlen die toch harmonieus samengaan door de gelijke afmetingen en hoogtes.

(*Above*) After crossing Bruges the Reie flowed formerly north to join a sea reach. In the 13th century the two banks at this spot were called the *Houtbrekersdam* or Wood Hewers dike as this is where the boatbuilders had their yards. Today the west bank is called the **Langerei** or Long Wharf and from the Spiegelrei on is lined with houses in various styles but of the same dimensions, creating a harmonious ensemble.

(*Ci-dessus*) Après avoir traversé Bruges, la Reie se dirigeait vers le nord pour rejoindre jadis le bras de mer. À cet endroit, les deux rives s'appelaient au XIIIᵉ siècle *Houtbrekersdam*, la «digue des briseurs de bois», car les constructeurs de navires y avaient établi leurs chantiers. Aujourd'hui, la rive ouest est le **Langerei** *(le long quai)* qui, à partir du spiegelrei, est bordé de maisons de styles différents mais dont l'équivalence des gabarits et de hauteur crée l'harmonie.

(*Oben*) Die Reie fließt, nachdem sie Brügge durchquert hat, gen Norden und mündet schließlich in den Meeresarm. An dieser Stelle wurden die beiden Flüsse im 13. Jahrhundert *Houtbrekersdam*, "Deich der Holzspalter", genannt, da die Bootsbauer dort ihre Werften errichtet hatten. Heute trägt das Westufer den Namen **Langerei** *(langer Kai)* und ist — ab der Spiegelrei — von Häusern in unterschiedlichen Stilrichtungen gesäumt, die jedoch aufgrund ihrer gleichartigen Formen und der einheitlichen Höhe ein harmonisches Gesamtbild abgeben.

(Volgende dubbele bladzijde)
De brug die sinds 1740 met haar drie bogen beide oevers van de Reie met elkaar verbindt, leidt tot de ingangspoort (1776) van het **begijnhof** "Ten Wijngaerde" in **Brugge** dat in 1245 door Margareta van Constantinopel werd gesticht. Vrome vrouwen wijdden er hun leven aan werk en gebed ; ze bereidden er o.a. wol voor de wevers. Na de dood van de laatste begijn in 1930 heeft een gemeenschap van benedictinessen de plaats van de begijnen ingenomen.

(Next two pages)
In **B**ruges, crossing the Reie, the three arches of this bridge, built in 1740, lead to the entrance portal (1776) of the **Béguine convent** called "the Vineyard". The convent, founded in 1245 by Margaret of Constantinople, housed pious women who devoted their time to prayer and work, notably preparing wool for weavers. When the last béguine died in 1930, a community of Benedictine nuns took over the convent.

(Double page suivante)
À **Bruges**, le pont qui, depuis 1740, franchit en trois arches la Reie mène au portail d'entrée (1776) du **béguinag**e de la Vigne fondé en 1245 par Marguerite de Constantinople. De pieuses femmes s'y vouaient à la prière et au travail ; elles préparaient notamment la laine pour les tisserands. Depuis 1930, année de la mort de la dernière béguine, une communauté de religieuses bénédictines a pris le relais.

(Nächste Doppelseite)
Die Brücke, die sich seit 1740 in drei Bögen über die Gracht spannt, führt zum Eingangsportal des 1245 von Margaretha von Konstantinopel ins Leben gerufenen und „Weinberg" genannten Beginenhofs in **Brügge**. Fromme Frauen widmeten sich dort dem Gebet und der Arbeit. Sie nahmen u. a. die Aufbereitung der Wolle für die Weber vor. Nachdem 1930 die letzte Begine verschieden war, hat eine Gemeinschaft von Benediktinerinnen das Stift übernommen.

◁

Lissewege, het dorp met de lage, gewitte en onderaan beteerde huizen, is uiterst typisch voor de Vlaamse kuststreek. De stoere toren met zijn vale roze tint werd, zoals de kerk zelf, in de 13de eeuw gebouwd. Hij is de laatste getuige van de rijke en machtige stad die zich toen hier uitstrekte. Naar het schijnt deed hij soms dienst als vuurtoren als er 's nachts storm op zee was.

Avec ses maisons basses aux briques soigneusement chaulées et aux soubassements goudronnés, le village de **Lissewege** est l'un des plus typiques de la Flandre maritime. Dernier témoin de son passé de ville riche et puissante, la robuste masse rose de la tour de son église du XIIIe siècle servait, semble-t-il, de phare les nuits de tempête.

The village of **Lissewege** with its low, whitewashed brick houses sitting on their tarred foundations, is typical of coastal Flanders. The sturdy, rose church tower (13th century), which served as a lighthouse on stormy nights, is the sole reminder of its rich and powerful past.

Mit seinen niedrigen, weißgekalkten, in Bodennähe geteerten Häusern ist **Lissewege** ein sehr charakteristisches Dorf des flämischen Küstengebietes. Der wuchtige, rosafarbene Turm der Kirche (13. Jh.) ist das letzte Baudenkmal, das an den Reichtum und die Macht der Stadt erinnert, die sich einst zu seinen Füßen ausbreitete. Früher, so scheint es, wurde er als Leuchtturm benutzt, wenn Schiffe nachts gegen den Sturm ankämpften.

△

Korte tijd nadat de *Hondsdam* was opgeworpen (1168), werd **Damme** de opslagplaats en de zeehaven van Brugge, dat voor de grote schepen niet meer bereikbaar was. De Hanze van Londen had er een factorij en de Lombarden een opslagplaats. Brugge was door een kanaal met Damme verbonden en, toen de verzanding van het Zwin verder gevorderd was, met Sluis, dat op zijn beurt aan de verzanding ten prooi viel.

Peu après l'achèvement de la *Digue du Chien* en 1168, **Damme** devint l'entrepôt commercial de Bruges devenue inaccessible aux navires de haute mer. La Hanse de Londres y établit un comptoir et les Lombards un dépôt. Un canal relié au Zwin assurait la communication entre Damme et Bruges. Mais l'ensablement gagna, à leur tour, Damme puis Sluis, et le canal perdit bientôt le chemin de l'océan...

Shortly after the completion of the *Dog's Dyke* in 1168, **Damme** became the trading entrepot for Bruges, no longer accessible to deep water ships. The London Hanse opened a branch and the Lombards a warehouse. A canal to the Zwin provided the connection between Damme and Bruges. But first Damme and then Sluis silted up and the canal could no longer reach the sea.

Nachdem der „Hondsdam" 1168 errichtet worden war, wurde Damme der Seehafen Brügges, das die Seeschiffe nicht mehr erreichten. Die Hanse von London und die Lombarden hatten Kontore in Damme. Ein zum Zwin führender Kanal verband Brügge mit Damme später mit Sluis, bis auch Sluis durch die fortschreitende Versandung vom Meer abgeschnitten wurde.

De oude zeehaven van **Oostende**, waar zeerovers en geuzen een schuilplaats hadden gevonden, vooraleer de vesting buiten gebruik werd gesteld, werd pas ten tijde van Leopold II de badstad bij uitstek. Het is tevens de grootste vissershaven van het land en de inschepings-plaats naar Dover. Ziehier hoe de passagiers de stad zien als ze opeengepakt op het dek van de uit Engeland komende ferry staan.

In de 18de eeuw was Oostende de thuishaven van de Indische Compagnie (later Oostendse Compagnie genoemd), waarvan de schepen de Chinese Zee en de golf van Bengalen bevoeren. Het oplei-dingsschip Mercator, dat sinds 1961 in de jachthaven voor anker ligt, had daarvoor eveneens alle wereldzeeën bevaren en havens van niet minder dan vierenvijftig landen aangedaan. Dat was nog in de tijd toen men ervan overtuigd was dat een zeilschip het ideale opleidings-schip voor toekomstige kapiteins en zeelui op lange vaart was.

In bygone days a haven for sailors, freebooters and seadogs, **Ostend** became the seaside resort par excellence under Leopold II. It is Belgium's largest fishing port and the crossing point for Dover. This is how it appears today to the passengers grouped on the deck of the ferry from England.

In the 18th century Ostend was the home port of our Indies Company whose sailing ships voyaged as far as the China Sea and the Bay of Bengal. Today the training ship "Mercator", wich has sailed the seven seas and made landfall in 54 different countries lies anchored before the yacht basin. It was long felt that the sailing ship provided the best training for a high seas mariner.

Vieille cité de marins, de flibustiers et de gueux, forteresse désaffec-tée, **Ostende** fut sous le règne de Léopold II la station balnéaire par excellence. Elle est aussi le plus grand port de pêche du pays et le point d'embarquement pour Douvres. Telle elle apparaît aujourd'hui aux passagers groupés sur le pont de la malle venue d'Angleterre.

Ostende fut, au XVIIIe siècle, le port d'attache des voiliers de notre Compagnie des Indes qui sillonnèrent les mers de Chine et du Bengale. Aujourd'hui, devant le port de plaisance, est ancré le navire-école «Mercator» qui a navigué sur toutes les mers du monde et fait escale dans cinquante-quatre pays différents. C'était au temps où l'on estimait que le voilier constitue le meilleur moyen de formation d'un marin au long cours.

Ostende war früher ein Unterschlupf für Seeräuber und Geusen sowie ein befestigter Schutzhafen. Leopold II. machte es zu einem mondänen Badeort. Heute ist Ostende der größte Fischereihafen Belgiens und ein Einschiffungsplatz nach Dover. Das Bild zeigt, wie die Passagiere die Stadt sehen, wenn sie Mann an Mann auf dem Deck des ankommenden Fährschiffs stehen.

Im 18. Jh. war Ostende der Heimathafen der Schiffe, die im Namen der Indischen Handelskompanie, der Handelskompanie von Ostende, auf den Chinesischen Meeren und im Golf von Bengalen segelten. Seit 1961 liegt im Jachthafen von Ostende das Schulschiff Mercator vor Anker. Zuvor war es ebenfalls auf allen Weltmeeren gesegelt und hatte in Häfen von vierundfünfzig verschiedenen Ländern angelegt. Damals dachte man noch, dass ein Segelschiff die beste Schule für einen angehenden Bewerber in der Hochseeschiffahrt sei.

◁◁

Aan het uiteinde van de 500 m lange pier, de brede wandeldijk van **Blankenberge**, ligt een achthoekig uitzichtterras. Het *Aquarama* bevat een zeldzame verzameling van schelpen en tevens een uitbeelding van het leven onder de zeespiegel.

Au bout de la digue-promenade de **Blankenberge**, les cinq cents mètres du *Pier* se terminent par une plate-forme octogonale. L'*Aquarama* y rassemble des coquillages rares et reconstitue les secrets de la vie sous-marine.

At the end of the sea wall promenade in **Blankenberge**, 500 meters of pier lead to an octagonal platform where the *Aquarama*, displaying the mysteries of marine life and a fine collection of shells, is situated.

Die 500 m lange Deichpromenade des *Pier* in **Blankenberge** endet auf einem achteckigen Platz. *Aquarama*, ein Aquarienhaus, zeigt seltene Muscheln und gibt ein eindrucksvolles Bild vom Leben unter dem Meeresspiegel.

△

De Haan is gelegen tussen Oostende en Blankenberge. Bij het ontstaan van deze badstad, op het eind van de 19de en het begin van de 20ste eeuw, werd veel aandacht besteed aan de eenheid in stijl van de gebouwen. De tramstation, gebouwd aan de vooravond van de Eerste Wereldoorlog, valt op door het speciale dak. Men vindt er invloeden terug terug van de Art nouveau, kenmerkend voor het eind van de Belle Epoque.

Station balnéaire située entre Ostende et Blankenberge, **Le Coq** (*De Haan*) s'est développée à la fin du XIXe siècle et au début du XXe, avec le souci de respecter une certaine unité de style des constructions. La gare de tramway, édifiée à la veille de la Première Guerre mondiale, surprend par le jeu de ses toits. On peut y déceler une certaine influence de l'Art Nouveau caractéristique de la fin de la Belle Epoque.

The seaside resort of **De Haan**, situated between Ostend and Blankenberge, was developed at the end of the 19th and in the early 20th centuries. Care was taken to ensure a certain harmony in the style of the buildings. The roof of the tramway terminus, built on the eve of World War I has rather unusual lines influenced by Art Nouveau as was often seen at the end of the Belle Epoque.

Seebad zwischen Ostende und Blankenberge, **De Haan** ist Ende des 19., Anfang des 20. Jhr. entstanden, wobei das Anliegen bestand, beim Stil der Bauwerke eine gewisse Einheitlichkeit zu wahren. Der kurz vor dem Ersten Weltkrieg erbaute Straßenbahn-Bahnhof überrascht durch das Spiel seiner Dächer. Es ist ein gewisser Art Nouveau-Einfluss zu erkennen, der für das Ende der Belle Epoque typisch ist.

◁

In 1918 bleef er van **Diksmuide** maar een grote puinhoop over. Later werd het marktplein in zijn oorspronkelijke staat hersteld en werd er in het stadhuis weer een beiaard met dertig klokken opgehangen. Ook de toren van de van 1543 daterende St.-Niklaaskerk vlak daarnaast werd weer opgebouwd. Eveneens ter nagedachtenis aan de tijdens Wereldoorlog I gesneuvelden werd er midden op het plein een monument ter ere van generaal baron Jacques de Dixmude opgericht.

En 1918, **Dixmude** se trouvait réduite à un amas de ruines. Sur la grand-place reconstruite dans son style d'origine, le nouvel hôtel de ville contient un carillon de trente cloches. Sa tour est voisine de celle — également reconstruite — de l'église Saint-Nicolas qui datait de 1536-1543. Au centre de la place, le monument du général baron Jacques de Dixmude rappelle le souvenir des combats de la Première Guerre mondiale.

In 1918 **Diksmuide** was only a heap of ruins. The new town hall on the main square, rebuilt in its original style, houses a thirty-bell carillon. Its tower is next to that of Saint Nicholas' church (1536-43), also rebuilt. In the center of the square stands a monument to General Baron Jacques de Dixmude, recalling the battles of the First World War.

1918 war **Diksmuide** nur noch eine einzige große Ruine. Danach wurde der Marktplatz wieder stilgetreu aufgebaut und vom Rathausturm erklang erneut das Glockenspiel mit seinen dreißig Glocken. Auch die nahe St.-Nikolauskirche und ihr Turm wurden neu aufgebaut. Mitten auf dem Platz steht das Standbild des Barons und Generals Jacques de Dixmude, das auch an die Schlachten des Ersten Weltkriegs erinnern soll.

△
Het belfort van **Ieper**, evenals de 350 m brede Lakenhalle zijn in hun vroegere glorie hersteld en waken over de stad, die haar voorspoed aan de lakennijverheid te danken had.

Rétablis dans leur gloire d'antan, le beffroi d'**Ypres** et les halles aux draps déployés sur trois cent cinquante mètres de pourtour veillent sur la ville qui doit sa prospérité première à l'industrie drapière.

Restored to their former glory, the Belfry of **Ypres** and the Cloth Hall, which measures close on 350 meters, watch over the city which first owed its prosperity to the cloth industry.

In ihrem einstmaligen Glanz wiederhergestellt, wachen der **Yperner Belfried** und die Tuchhallen auf einer Breite von 350 Metern über die Stadt, die ihren ersten Wohlstand der Tuchindustrie verdankte.

▷
Kortrijk heeft zijn roem aan de lakennijverheid te danken. Het Sint-Elisabeth begijnhof, één van de meest aantrekkelijke hofjes in Vlaanderen, doet ons denken aan de dichter Guido Gezelle, die van 1871 tot 1899 kapelaan was van de Onze-Lieve-Vrouwekerk.

Courtrai devait sa renommée à l'industrie drapière. Son béguinage Sainte-Elisabeth, l'un des plus séduisants de Flandre, rappelle le souvenir du poète Guido Gezelle qui, de 1871 à 1899, fut vicaire à l'église Notre-Dame.

Courtrai owes its fame to the cloth industry. Its beguinage of Saint Elisabeth, one of the most attractive in Flanders, recalls memories of the poet Guido Gezelle, who was a vicar here, at the church of Our Lady, from 1871 to 1899.

Kortrijk verdankte seinen Ruf der Tuchweberei. Sein Beginenhof der Heiligen Elisabeth, einer der reizvollsten Flanderns, weckt die Erinnerung an den Dichter Guido Gezelle, der 1871-1899 Vikar der Liebfrauenkirche war.

✿ VINCENT MERCKX

E D I T I O N S

www.meditio.com

2006 © Editions Merckx Uitgeverij s.p.r.l. b.v.b.a.
Avenue des Statuaires 145A Beeldhouwerslaan, B-1180 Bruxelles Brussel
☎ +32/2/374.41.56 • Fax +32/2/375.80.37

Photographs
Vincent Merckx

Photoassistant
Philippe Molitor

Texts
Georges-Henri Dumont

Nederlandse bewerking & Deutsche Übersetzung
DSDB

English translation
Sheila Tessier-Lavigne

Printing
Daneels Group

D-1998-0398-19
ISBN 90-74847-19-6

Bij dezelfde uitgever
Chez le même éditeur
By the same publisher
In demselben Verlag

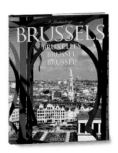

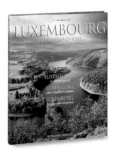

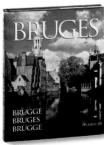